MW00620953

A Levittown Legacy

© 2019 by Gary Gray
Photographs ©2019 Little League Baseball, Incorporated, All Rights
Reserved: Cover photos, pages 26, 168, 169, 172, 174

All other photos from Gary Gray's personal archives; clippings from
the Bucks County Courier Times (page 41) and the Centre Daily Times
(pages 65,59,73, 75, 133)

Printed in the United States of America

All rights reserved. This publication is protected by Copyright, and
permission should be obtained from the publisher prior to any prohibited
reproduction, storage in a retrieval system, or transmission in any form
or by any means, electronic, mechanical, photocopying, recording, or
likewise.

Published by Mt. Nittany Press,
an imprint of Eifrig Publishing,
PO Box 66, Lemont, PA 16851.
Knobelsdorffstr. 44, 14059 Berlin, Germany

For information regarding permission, write to:
Rights and Permissions Department,
Eifrig Publishing,
PO Box 66, Lemont, PA 16851, USA.
permissions@eifrigpublishing.com, 888-340-6543.

Library of Congress Cataloging-in-Publication Data

Gray, Gary
A Levittown Legacy: 1960 Little League Baseball World Champions,
by Gary Gray
p. cm.

Paperback:	ISBN 978-1-63233-233-2
Hardcover:	ISBN 978-1-63233-234-9
Ebook:	ISBN 978-1-63233-235-6

    1. Memoir 2. Baseball 3. History - Sport History
I. Gray, Gary II. Title.

23 22 21 20 2019
5 4 3 2 1

Printed on acid-free paper. ∞

A Levittown Legacy:

1960 Little League Baseball World Champions

by Gary J. Gray

Mt. Nittany Press
Lemont, PA

Acknowledgments

To Katie O'Toole—*my loving wife and journalistic critic who makes every written phrase better with her comments.*

To Terry Nau, Levittown sports writer and friend for putting me in touch with the players from the 1960 and 1961 Levittown American All-Star teams, and his comments on the earlier stages of the book.

To the 1960 Cheerleaders (Ladies First) who shared their stories with me: Louise Bellavita (Vieth), Cathy Bellavita (Richardson), and Marion Amoroso. The three other cheerleaders were: Jody Gervasi, Patty Reilly and Eileen Kaufman.

To the players on the 1960 and 1961 teams who responded to my call for insight in telling their story: Julian Kalkstein, Joe Fioravanti, Tucker Schwartz, Roger Barto, Jim Grauel, and Dennis Pesci. A particular thank you to Craig Eisenhart who provided me with many photos and stories about both the 1960 and 61 teams.

A special shout-out to Steve Amoroso who did me a very great favor in giving me an in-depth background on the coaches of the 1960 team, and he also provided me with some photos and stories about the 1960 season.

Table of Contents

Author's Note

I am a teaching professor at Penn State University, where I received my Ph.D. in Finance. After a 15-year stint on Wall Street, where I was a Managing Director of Lehman Brothers and Senior Vice President for E.F. Hutton, two now bankrupt investment banks, I came back to Penn State to co-teach, with Professor J. Randall Woolridge, the beginning Finance 301 course in the Smeal College of Business. It is a required core business course, and I teach over 2,500 business students per year.

I am the author or co-author of numerous finance books and academic papers, including *Streetsmart Guide to Valuing a Stock,* printed by McGraw Hill and co-authored by Patrick Cusatis and Randy Woolridge. This book has been translated into Chinese and is in a second edition. I also am an author, along with Patrick Cusatis, of *Municipal Derivative Securities: Uses and Valuation*, published by Irwin Professional Publishing. I am also the author of a fun memoir, *Running with the Bulls: Fiestas, Corridas, Toreros and an American's Adventures in Pamplona*, published by Lyons Press, where I describe my travels and exploits over a 30-year time period of running with the bulls of Pamplona, Spain.

I attended Penn State on a football scholarship and was a Penn State Linebacker back in the late 60's to early 70's. In Chapter 2, I bring Penn State into the picture, specifically "The Immaculate Reception" of Franco Harris, my college roommate for three years. Head PSU Football Coach Joe Paterno is also introduced, along with Frank Sinatra, who makes an appearance singing with my mother, a cabaret singer, at one of her Trenton gigs—although I don't think Sinatra was a Penn State graduate.

As a source for much of my material on the beginnings and politics of Little League Baseball, I relied on the book, *Play Ball-The Story of Little League Baseball*, written by Lance and Robin Van Aukin, that was published by the Penn State Press. I also used ancient newspaper articles sourced through Newspaper.com to follow the box scores and daily depiction of the 1960 and 1961 All Star playoff games—each of which occurred very long ago.

So, during the rise of Levittown American in 1960, I was a ten-year old catcher in the Levittown National Little League. Vicariously, I enjoyed living through the 1960 Levittown American team players who won the Little League Baseball World Championship.

Please read on and I hope that you become a Levittown American fan!

Chapter 1

The Creation of Little League Baseball

Almost 60 years later, Craig Eisenhart can distill into a single word the most important lesson he learned from the biggest game of his life. "Teamwork."

Baseball is a sport of so many moving parts. Each baseball game begins with a home team player's first wind up and delivery from the pitcher's mound. The game ends with the losing team's final out. If your teammates are in rhythm, it will likely be a good day for your team on the baseball diamond. If the players are out of sync and playing just to improve their own statistics, your team is likely to lose.

It might seem obvious with the perspective of six decades, but trying to get noticed in a crowded and competitive athletic environment your goal is rarely to be a cog no matter how well-oiled the machine might be. Eisenhart learned the lesson game by game over a remarkable season in 1960. That year there were over 5,500 Little Leagues world-wide. Every league was invited to pick an "All-Star" team that would compete in a baseball tournament to eventually become the Little League Baseball World Series Champions. The tournament in 1960 was single-elimination. One loss and the season was over. The goal of each Little League all-star team was to win all of its games. Clearly, only one of the 5,500 teams would reach the goal. Every all-star player wanted that one team to be his.

The Levittown American team won thirteen consecutive games. The probability of winning that number of games against teams of equal talent is not high, only about 1 in 10,000. My maternal grandfather was a bookie in 1960. He wouldn't have given good odds to the Levittown Americans.

Nevertheless, the tournament is structured so that only one team will succeed in being undefeated and in winning the Little League World Championship. This is a memoir that focuses on the 1960 Little League All-Star Baseball World Series and the Levittown American team that won it. I was 10 years old at the time, and I closely followed and cheered on the rise of the Levittown American All-Stars. They were 17 extremely talented eleven- and twelve-year old boys who won all of their games against all-star baseball teams from throughout the United States and the world to become the 1960 Little League Baseball World Series Champions.

Levittown American had more talent than an average Little League All-Star team. They won all of their games, and they did it with poise, athleticism and superb coaching. Skillful players manned every position and their talent was manifest in the pitching of Julian Kalkstein, Joe Mormello, Tucker Schwartz, and Craig Eisenhart; the hitting of Joe Fioravanti, Chet Gardner, Jim Grauel, Brian Pennington, Jim Fleming, and Mark Griffith; the fielding of Rollie Clark, Rodger Barto, and Donald Bickel; and the backup support of alternates, Dave Lenhart, Harry Cramer, and Chuck McCabe.

Levittown American could also make a claim that probably no other baseball team—*Major League, Minor League, or Little League*—had ever accomplished. The team was never behind its opponent at the end of any inning during the entire all-star tournament. That's 78 consecutive innings in which Levittown American never had to come from behind to win a baseball game.

Part of this success may have been due to Coach William Dvorak's unusual decision to always be the visiting team. That contrasts with the strategy of most baseball teams. If a team wins the coin toss, its coaches almost always want to bat last to have that final chance to come from behind and win the game. Dvorak had confidence in Levittown's first four or five batters (Kalkstein, Gardner, Fioravanti, Mormello, Grauel). He counted on them to start the games off with some hits or home runs and immediately force their opponents into playing catch-up baseball. Trailing an opponent creates unease and puts young 11 and 12-year-old players in a defensive position from the start. Pressure your opponent early in the game? Dvorak may have been onto something.

Levittown American's top two pitchers, Joe Mormello and Julian Kalkstein, tossed several no-hitters and a half dozen one- and two- hitters. They overpowered batters while chalking up an enormous number of strike outs. Mormello struck out 89% of the batters that he faced during the tournament.

As Craig Eisenhart told me, "With Mormello or Kalkstein on the mound, very early in the all-star tournament, our team believed we had a real opportunity to win it all and to be standing in Williamsport in late August basking in the cheers of the crowd and in the warm summer sun."

But it was going to take more than confidence to get to Williamsport.

Williamsport Here We Come

In the early morning of Saturday, August 27 in 1960, we began a four-hour long journey to Williamsport-- my dad, Edward Gray, our next-door neighbor, Leon Novak, and I. We left our home in Levittown in the southeastern corner of Pennsylvania for a baseball game that would be played that afternoon near the center of the state. Williamsport was about 180 miles from Levittown. I was 10 years old, and besides driving to the New Jersey shore a couple of times, I had never traveled very far from home.

Six decades later, I remember it as a long trip—the US Interstate Highway System had not yet been completed and we travelled over some bumpy two-lane roads. My father drove our silver Chevy Impala and my Uncle Leon accompanied us and navigated. Uncle Leon was not a blood uncle, but he was our next-door neighbor and my dad's best friend. He was married to "Aunt" Lucille. In a pop-up community like Levittown, the labelling of neighbors as aunts and uncles was one way to create a sense of extended family.

Sports was another.

My family lived in the Greenbrook section of Levittown on Garden Lane right next to the Novak family. The adjoining backyards of the Gray and Novak houses were our first sports arena. My dad, my sister Bonnie, and I would play baseball, kick ball, soft ball, and basketball—we had a backboard and a hoop in the driveway, and we would play against Uncle Leon, his daughter Linda, and his two younger sons, Leon Jr. (nicknamed Bo), and his brother, Clint. Neither my mother nor Aunt Lucille were very athletic, and they were content to watch our backyard games.

A typical Levittown house

On that August day we were likewise happy to be spectators, cheering on our otherwise baseball rival—the Levittown American All-Stars. Rooting for Levittown American did not come easily for me. At age 10, I was too young and not yet good enough to play for the National All-Stars, the Levittown league that the Greenbrook boys funneled into. But my personal interest in cheering against a local rival was easily suppressed by the community pride that a Levittown team was headed for the final world series championship game. I figured that next year I could be playing against some of these 11-year-old Levittown American guys, so it was also a scouting trip of sorts for me. I was going to take the measure of my future opponents. And I would check out the ballpark where I planned to be in 1961. For every Little Leaguer, it was the Field of Dreams in Williamsport, Pennsylvania— the birthplace of Little League Baseball.

Uncle Leon was a bit shorter than my dad but more compact and he had curly black hair. He was a high-power mechanic at a manufacturing company and he operated and repaired various types of machinery in areas near Levittown. He was a very can-do guy and a bit of a prankster, but he was a good person and often would help my dad with our team's baseball practices.

My dad died twenty years later at the age of 60. In the excitement of throwing a strike in his much beloved morning bowling league, he collapsed on the alley and never recovered. Despite the heart attack that killed him quickly, I'm almost sure he had a smile on his face.

My dad was even more generous in his support for the rival coaches. He was a hands-on father and he coached my Little League baseball teams throughout my early years. He was a pretty good athlete himself with a frame of 5 feet 11 inches and a thin but muscular body. He pitched batting practice to me and my teammates and he spent many weekends and evenings with me on the baseball fields of Levittown.

Levittown baseball field

In a recent conversation with one of my old teammates, David Schaeffer, he told me about my dad's coaching and teaching skills, "Your father had a very big positive influence on my life," Schaeffer said. His words could not have made me happier and I was proud of my dad.

In 1960, I played catcher for Meenan Oil, our corporate sponsor in the Levittown National's Major League. The National League in 1960 consisted of approximately 250 boys. Little League Baseball had not yet permitted girls to play.

Levittown had five Little Leagues. And playing in a specific league was based on the neighborhood or section where the player lived. National League players, like me, came from blue-collar sections such as Greenbrook, Farmbrook, or Stonybrook. Boys from the American League lived in the more upscale sections of Birch Valley, Magnolia Hill, North Park, Elderberry, Vermillion Hills, and Thornridge.

Besides the National and American Leagues, Levittown had the International League, the Continental League, and the Western League. There were eleven other leagues in Lower Bucks County, close to Levittown that, along with the Levittown teams, were part of Pennsylvania District 21 of Little League Baseball. Those 11 non-Levittown leagues were: Council Rock, Pennridge, Fairless Hills, Bristol Township, Pennsbury National, Bristol Borough, Pennsbury American, Bristol Township American, Bristol Township National, Trevose, and the Morrisville Little League. The Morrisville team was the Lower Bucks County team that had won this same Little League World Series championship five years earlier in 1955.

These leagues kept 250 to 300 boys, ages eight to twelve very busy during their summers. Age and talent determined which team a boy would join in any given league. And each league had teams that were composed of boys who had been sorted by their age and abilities. The *Major League*—was at the top of the food chain with the most highly skilled 10- to 12-year-olds. *The Minor League*— had the less talented 9- to 11-year-old players. The *Pee-Wee League* was for 8- to 9-year-olds, who were developing players.

A substantial time commitment was required from a player to participate in Little League, and it may have been a key reason that juvenile delinquency seemed to me to be rare in Lower Bucks County in the 1960s. All of my friends played Little League Baseball, and none of them was a hooligan.

The Odds: Want to Place a Bet on the All-Star Game?

The odds of a particular team winning a baseball tournament with 5,500 Little League All-Star teams competing are not good. My Grandfather, Morris Gottlieb, was Jewish and he could have told anyone about the odds. He was a good professional gambler at the card table, but he really made his living by winning bets from less informed sports fans. He bet strictly with the odds and was happy with receiving "the vigorish," otherwise known as the profit margin.

Grandpop Gottlieb was powerfully built with a deep husky voice, and he looked like he could handle himself in a street fight. Bookmakers at that time had to stay on the good side of the Police Department and contribute generously to their local politicians. Grandpop had an office in center city Philadelphia where the card games were played and sports bets were taken. Card games were another way for a professional bookie to take advantage of the rookie.

The Quest of the Little Leaguers

In 1960, the rule for every Little League Baseball all-star team was: **WIN AND PLAY ON; LOSE AND GO HOME.** Winning the Little League World Championship truly was a *Survival of the Fittest*, and it was a very big deal.

For teams from densely-packed areas like Levittown, it was a challenge just to get beyond the local level, to become the District 21 champion. Levittown, with its five leagues, is an example of an area with a ton of talent and where the players competed locally with the hope of moving onto state, then regional and then national contests.

Many times, some potentially very good all-star teams have been knocked out of the tournament prematurely in the Local Division as their coaches were just weaving their talented players together into a team. The first few steps of the Little League World Series were to beat the all-star teams from the rival Levittown leagues and the other leagues that were members of Pennsylvania District 21 and become Local Champions.

In 1960, Pennsylvania was divided into four league sections. The Levittown area was in Section 4 which encompassed the Southeast portion of the state. The Sectional or State Champion would need to defeat teams from the other three Sections around Pennsylvania to become the Sectional or State Champions.

Next, Levittown would face other state champs from the Northeastern region of the United States including New York, New Jersey and the New England states to become the Regional Champions.

The Regional Champs were the eight teams from around the world that were still alive with an unblemished 10-0 record. These teams would each aim to win the last three games in Williamsport, where they would compete against the other unbeaten champions. Only one team could survive this grueling gauntlet of games, to be crowned the World Champions of Little League Baseball.

Levittown American had already won the first two of its three games in Williamsport. We were now travelling to see that final game, and hoping that number thirteen would not prove to be an unlucky number for Levittown.

Exactly What is a Levittown?

The name *Levittown* is a misnomer because it is not really a town or a city or a borough. It consists of fragments of three townships in Lower Bucks County – Bristol, Falls, and Middletown, and the Borough of Tulleytown. It is located about 15 miles north and east of Philadelphia and only a couple of hundred yards from the Delaware River.

Levittown is a census-designated place (CDP), which is an area without well-defined boundaries,

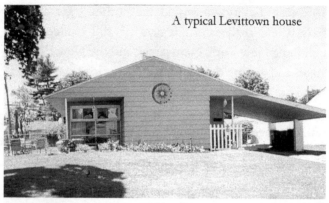

A typical Levittown house

and it did not exist in 1950 when I was born. A CDP has a concentration of population in communities that resemble cities but lack incorporation or any type of municipal government. Construction of Levittown began in early 1952. In creating Levittown, the developers William Levitt and his brother Alfred, designed and built six models of single-family houses and used an assembly line-like process in the construction of the homes.

My family lived in the most basic and least expensive Levittown model which sold for $9,900. Home buyers could also choose the Jubilee for $11,990, the Pennsylvanian for $14,500, or the Country Clubber for $17,500.

The Levitts capitalized on providing homes for families of military veterans who were returning from World War II duty and who were looking to live in an atmosphere that would be attractive to families on a tight budget. The developers understood that bargain-priced housing would be popular among couples who were starting families now that World War II had ended.

The return of so many soldiers from the battlefields of Europe and Asia meant an instant market for affordable homes. The Levitts expected the houses to sell like hotcakes, and they did. The Levitts also benefitted in 1952 from a decision of the United States Steel Company to build a new huge steel making facility in nearby Fairless Hills. It employed a large number of young mill workers, and many of the returning servicemen found jobs there.

More than 15,000 single-family homes were quickly sold by the Levitt Brothers with no down payment required for veterans. The government also had programs that guaranteed low interest rate mortgages that were designed for veterans to finance and purchase a home.

Levittown in the 1950s and 1960s seemed to me like an ideal place to raise a young family. In retrospect, it was ideal only for families with certain demographics.

Before anyone could purchase a house in Levittown, the applicants had to agree to sign onto and abide by the *Levitt Rules*, which were spelled out in a pamphlet. Some of the rules were similar to those of today's neighborhood associations. "As a homeowner: you are obligated to cut your grass at least once a week; you are not permitted to fence your property; and you can't hang laundry outside on weekends or holidays."

Other rules were less innocuous. Homeowners were forbidden to sell or resell to persons that are: "… other than members of the Caucasian race." The Levitt family would not sell the homes to racial minorities, nor would they allow subsequent owners of Levittown homes to resell to members of those minorities.

Consequently, I grew up in a light-skinned community with little to no African/American, Latino, or Asian influence. Very few non-Caucasian students attended my Catholic grade school and Catholic high school, and none played on my Little League Baseball teams.

Lone Star State Versus Keystone State

As we arrived at the Little League complex in Williamsport, we were stunned by the crowd of about 15,000 who were there to watch the final game between Levittown American and Fort Worth, Texas. Several of the Texas fans were wearing 10-gallon hats, and I thought they looked pretty funny.

The front-page article of the August 28, 1960 edition of the *Williamsport Grit* headlined, "Crowd of 15,000 sees L.L. Championship Tilt."

"The largest crowd ever to attend a Little League Baseball World Series game filled the stand of Howard J. Lamade Memorial Field and spilled over to the surrounding banks to watch the championship game.

"Countless hundreds of thousands of others throughout the nation were watching the game on their television screens by way of a special coast-to-coast hook-up. If this was the most looked at Little League series game in history, it was also one of the most exciting.

"Before the game got under way, a portly Texan, wearing a 10-gallon hat, led a group of fans in singing *The Yellow Rose of Texas*."

At the same time, on the other side of the field Levittown's girl cheerleaders were leading their fans in a cheer for the Pennsylvania team.

All the elements were in place for a thrilling duel between the Lone Star State and the Keystone State. Little League Baseball had come a long way from the improvised game played on empty lots and village greens.

Professional Baseball
Roots of Little League Baseball

Before there was Little League baseball, there was Major League Baseball. That's not what it was called by the New York Knickerbockers, the social baseball club whose members are credited with the first set of modern rules for a sport derived from the British game of Rounders.

Baseball in the United States had been developing in New York since June 1846 when the New York Knickerbocker Baseball Team met the New York Baseball Club in a game played in Hoboken, New Jersey. The initial rules, foul lines, and shape of the field were established in 1847. A decade later, the National Association of Base Ball Players was formed and the sport was fine-tuned. Baseball was now an official sport.

Professional baseball struggled in its early years. In 1876, the National League was born, and the rival American League was founded 25 years later. Until this time, baseball had not been an overwhelming financial success.

Byron "Ban" Johnson is credited with founding the American Baseball League and starting competition with the National Baseball League. By trying to lure top players away from the National League, he started a two-year player bidding war between leagues. His ultimate stroke of brilliance was the development of an end-of-season contest between the winners of the two Leagues—the original "Baseball World Series."

As professional baseball became more and more popular, cities and towns began to establish baseball teams for boys. Athletically-minded parents, educators, and youth groups began developing sports teams for younger boys. Several factors played into the rise of team sports at the high school, collegiate, and community levels. One was a concern about the health and physical fitness of American youth. The Industrial Revolution had lured countless strapping young men off the farms and into factories and office jobs. Sociologists and health care experts believed the lack of sunshine, fresh air, and manual labor was turning American men into pale, weak shadows of the robust farm boy image.

A second factor was the deluge of immigrants in the post-civil war era. Arriving in droves in US cities and speaking a Babel of languages, young immigrants found a sense of belonging on teams that often formed along ethnic lines.

In addition, youth sports teams were considered an antidote for juvenile delinquency. In time, some communities viewed youth sports as a value-add that would attract new residents.

Social entities such as the hundreds of Young Men's Christian Association (YMCA) chapters got behind the boys' baseball movement. New York City also became involved, and its YMCA sponsored and developed a 30-team league in 1889. This was an early model for Little Leagues.

But recruiting a team and playing a game was easy. The players then needed to have land on which to build a baseball field. Cities began to set aside land for recreational use. The builders of Levittown knew this well and followed that same formula. During the 1950s and 1960s, it seemed to me like the social life for boys in Levittown revolved around the baseball diamonds, basketball courts, and football fields that were built by the Levitt Brothers.

The growth of baseball teams, especially in the Northeast United States, became so significant that young players clamored for clubs of their own. As the nation was climbing out of the Great Depression in the 1930's, a doting uncle in Williamsport, Pennsylvania, answered the clamor of his two nephews.

Lance and Robin Van Auken, in their book, "Play Ball! The Story of Little League Baseball," have chronicled the history of Little League Baseball. They credit Carl Stotz as the driving force behind its birth. Stotz was a fan of professional baseball, a passion shared by his two young nephews—Jimmy Gehron, age 6, and Harold "Major" Gehron, age 8. The Gehron Brothers often joined Stotz in the stands to watch the games of the local professional minor league team, the Williamsport Grays. Uncle Carl also played baseball with his nephews and their friends.

One day, Stotz set up a training session to knock the ball around and gauge how serious the interest was among potential players for a baseball league devoted solely to 8- to 12-year-old boys. Stotz realized that the major league baseball dimensions were too big for young players. He solved that problem by shrinking everything by about one-third. The distance between bases on a standard field was 90 feet and he reduced it to 60 feet for younger boys. And he shortened the pitching distance to home plate from 60 feet to 46 feet.

Stotz continued to experiment that summer to fine-tune both the structure and the rules of youth baseball. If his program was to work properly, it would require

Carl Stotz and
some little leaguers

local sponsorship, plenty of volunteers and someone to contribute money to pay for the bats, balls, gloves, uniforms, baseball fields and the umpires. There would also be ongoing maintenance costs. Someone had to cut the grass, level the dirt, chalk the field lines, and paint the bleachers.

Stotz was persistent. His first league was comprised of three teams. He coached one team. His friend, George Bebble, coached a second team, and Bebble's brother, Bert, took on the third.

The City of Williamsport offered a site that could be turned into a baseball field. Stotz told his employer that he would name one of the teams Lundy Lumber, if he would agree to sponsor the team by making a $30 contribution. Other businesses likewise lent their names to teams: Lycoming Dairy and Jumbo Pretzel. Stotz called his three-team association, the "Little League."

The first Little League game was played on June 6, 1939, between Lycoming Dairy and Lundy Lumber. Lundy outscored Lycoming 23 to 8—a veritable trouncing. Across the 16-game schedule over the summer, the other game scores tended to be much closer. Lycoming Dairy came in second with 8 wins and 8 losses, a 50%, record; Lundy Lumber topped the league with a record of 9-7, 56%; and Jumbo Pretzel finished the season in last place was 7-9, a 44% record. The close game scores and win/loss records of the teams reflected a figurative leveling of the playing field as the rules were codified and game strategies were developed.

The playoff in 1939 pitted the champion of the first half of the season against the second-half champion in a best of 5-game series. Lycoming won the first half, with Carl Stotz managing, and Lundy Lumber won the second half. Lycoming Dairy beat Lundy Lumber 3 games to 2 in the 5-game 1939 playoff.

This brief baseball series was popular enough that it continued the following year, adding more teams. Other cities took note and followed Williamsport's example. By 1960, there were 27,400 Little League teams in 5,500 Little Leagues around the world including five leagues in Levittown, a town that didn't even exist in 1939 when Little League began. Levittown would prove to be so fertile for sports that it would produce a world championship team within a decade of its founding.

The 1960 Rules of Little League Baseball (Condensed Version)

The Little League Official 1960 Rules and Regulations booklet, which sold for 10 cents ($0.10), outlined the dos and don'ts of the game if the league was part of Little League baseball. As the news about the Little League spread across the country to other cities and towns like Levittown, adults and children wanted to adopt a program that would make baseball more of a sport that could be played by young boys—something that was desperately needed with the Baby Boom due to the ending of the second world war.

The rules were designed to promote a level playing field. Local teams were limited to a roster of 12 to 15 players, that included no more than 6 twelve-year old's, and at least 2 ten-year old's.

Players had to provide proof of age—a birth certificate or hospital record. The concern was that one or several youthful-looking teenagers might be added by an unscrupulous coach to the playoff roster for a Little League All-Star team.

There was also a non-residence requirement that prohibited players from switching to another league to be eligible to play on a particular all-star team. This limitation is designed to prohibit players from switching from one local league, in which he is a resident, to another league, in which he is not a resident but may be living with a relative or friend to be eligible to play on a particular league's all-star team.

Girls were not eligible.

The Eligibility Affidavit for the 1960 Levittown American League All-Star Team lists the players, street address, date of birth, and regular season team, and is signed by: John R. Mack, President of Levittown American Little League (see Appendix 2).

What happens if and when you break the rules?

The two major concerns about eligibility are Age and Residence. In the 1992 Little League World Series, the Far East representative was from Zamboanga City in the Philippines. The team used ineligible imported players, due to residence outside of the eligible area, to win the championship against Long Beach, California, by the score of 15-4. When the rule violation was uncovered, Long Beach was declared the winner with a score of 6-0, and the Philippines had a very embarrassing forfeit.

The exclusion of girls from Little League was barely an issue in the 1960s. Girls had softball leagues and the occasional young lady who wanted to pursue baseball was regarded as an oddity. The first girl known to have played Little League Baseball was Kathryn Johnston-Massar from Corning, New York. She went by the nickname of "Tubby." She posed as a boy and played for King's Dairy in 1951. She cut her hair short, dressed like a boy, and made the team, earning the coveted first baseman position. She played well, and part way into the season, she confided to her coach that she was a girl. He said she was a good player and was welcomed to stay. The Little League Board of Directors disagreed and she was kicked out of Little League baseball. The Little League Administrators then created the "Tubby Rule" which stated simply, "Girls are not eligible under any circumstances."

Subsequently, the Women's Movement in the 1960s and the Title Nine debates of the early 1970s led to the demise of stipulations like the Tubby Rule. In 1974, girls were finally allowed to play Little League Baseball, after contesting that position in numerous and costly court cases over the years. Still, not many girls try out to play on Little League baseball teams. The Van Aukens note that the Little League Softball program grew from approximately 30,000 players in 1974, the year the ban was dropped, to more than 390,000 players when their book was published in 2001.

As far as talent goes, a girl from Philadelphia, Mo'ne Davis, became the first girl to pitch a shutout and win a Little League World Series All-Star game. She played for the Taney Dragons of Philadelphia and she scored a 4-0 victory over South Nashville in 2014. She had proven to be a popular player. She was African American and had received encouragement from then President Barack Obama and his wife, Michelle. In 2015, Mo'ne, along with Hilary Beard, released a memoir, *Mo'ne Davis: Remember my name; My Story from First Pitch to Game Changer.*

Chapter 2

Growing Up in Levittown—
The 1950's and 1960's

In the early 1950s, farmers were growing potatoes, wheat, and corn in the Bucks County fields that would soon become Levittown. Located about 20 miles northeast of Philadelphia, those fields were about to be transformed into suburbia thanks to the vision of the Levitt family. In 1929, Abraham Levitt had established the house construction and development firm, Levitt & Sons. His younger son, Alfred, became the chief architect while the older son, William, inherited the presidency of the real estate company.

During the Second World War, William Levitt served in the Navy in the Seabees where he learned to mass produce military housing using standard and interchangeable parts. Upon his return to America, his expertise served him well. With the end of the war, hundreds of thousands of returning veterans were searching for affordable housing.

The Levitts saw an opportunity to provide an alternative to cramped city row homes and apartments. The developers understood their market. They mass produced bargain-priced, detached single-family homes with modern kitchen appliances and tidy moderate-sized lawns for families who were on a tight budget. They built their instant communities in attractive settings with open spaces where residents could walk, bike, and play. Playgrounds, parks and other outdoor facilities dotted their developments.

The Levittown Public Recreational Association (LPRA) constructed and administered the five Olympic-sized swimming pools and adjacent basketball courts that were built in and around Levittown. Country Club Pool was situated between Forsythia Gate and Snowball Gate. Pinelake Pool was built between the sections of Pinewood and Lakeside. Brook Pool was at the intersection of Greenbrook, Stonybrook, and Farmbrook. Magnolia Pool was built in Magnolia Park, and Indian Creek Pool was located in Indian Creek.

A playground in Levittown

My house had easy access to Brook Pool, to outdoor basketball courts that could also be used for stickball, and to the John Fitch Elementary School. Best of all, three Little League baseball diamonds were connected to the John Fitch school. They were only a stone's throw away and easily in the range of my bicycle. On these fields, I transitioned from pee-wee to pony league, to minor league, to the National Baseball League, where I became the catcher on the 1962 Little League All-Star team. Unfortunately, our All-Star team flamed out very early in that tournament.

The model for Pennsylvania's Levittown had already been Beta-tested in New York. The first Levittown was built on Long Island, and it became the archetype for the post-war suburbs. William Levitt, who is widely regarded as the "Father of Suburbia," drew upon his Seabee experience to devise an efficient 26-step process for building a home. He did not believe in labor unions, so he paid his non-union workers competitive wages and offered them incentives such as generous overtime pay. He did not like to pay middlemen and he ordered his parts directly from manufacturers. As a result, he was able to sell his houses in the early 1950s for as little as $8,000 each.

Demand for Levitt's Long Island houses soon outpaced the supply, and construction of the second Levittown began in February of 1952 in Lower Bucks County. The construction of each home was organized in an assembly-line manner where teams of workers did specific jobs, like plastering, roofing, or flooring. The builders moved from house to house as their part

John Fitch Elementary
School in Levittown

in the process was finished. Using this technique, when the workers were at the top of their game, they finished a house every hour. When the planned community was completed in 1958, more than 17,000 homes had been built.

The houses were laid out in 41 distinct neighborhoods of detached single-family homes. The Levitts donated eight or nine parcels of land at some of the intersections of those neighborhoods. Schools, churches, swimming pools, parks, and baseball fields were built on these grounds. The Levitts also promoted good landscaping practices. Knowing that many home buyers were from cities where row homes had no yards or very small ones, the Levitts provided guidelines on lawn and tree care to residents. Such attention to details large and small enhanced the curb appeal of the homes and added to the sense that Levittown was an attractive, self-contained, and safe community for raising a family.

The price of a Levittown home was right for the many young families like mine who descended on Levittown. The Levitts catered to war veterans, like my

Dad. Vets were not required to make a down payment on their home purchase. Also, war veterans could receive a government-guaranteed, low interest rate mortgage, specifically designed to finance the homes. With no down payment requirement and a government guaranteed low-rate mortgage for a home, a "Levittowner" model fit squarely into the price range of men like my father. He had served in the Navy during World War II, and he was employed with a reasonable salary, but he had no significant nest egg to make the down payment typically required of home buyers.

The Levitts rapidly built and sold 15,000 single-family homes. Like my Dad, many young men who had recently returned from World War II were marrying their sweethearts and collectively launching the baby boom. Most Levittown families were first-time home buyers, and many of them already had one or two children.

The typical Levittown home buyers had grown up in Philadelphia or across the Delaware River in either Trenton or Camden in New Jersey, or were from the Pittsburgh area moving to the location of the new US Steel Mill in Fairless Hills, and they were not accustomed to the grassy open spaces around a detached single-family home. For most of their lives, they had lived on meager budgets, initially due to the economic hardship of the Great Depression, then by the deprivations and sacrifices of World War Two. In the post-war period, the economy, like the youth population, boomed. At last, couples were ready to splurge on homes of their own that they would fill with children.

My Family

Both my mother and father had grown up in the confined and crowded spaces of row homes in northeast Philadelphia. They eagerly embraced detached homeownership, even with the grass mowing, leaf raking, and snow shoveling that it entailed.

In 1952, when I was two-years old, we were prime candidates for a move to Levittown. The new suburb was only 15 miles from my Grandmom and Grandpop Gottlieb's row home on 6331 Leonard Street in Northeast Philadelphia where my parents

SEPTEMBER 1957

ST. MICHAEL'S SCHOOL
1959-60

had been living in since I was born. The Gottlieb home also had accommodated my Great Aunt Gertie Bryan, the sister of my Grandmom Gottlieb, and my Aunt Rose Marie, my mother's sister. My Uncle Eugene Bryan also lived in the house.

My grandfather, Morris Gottlieb, supported our extended family through his high-risk successes as a bookie. He was always good to me. Together we watched professional baseball and football games on TV, cheering on the team whose victory or spread would make my grandpop the most money. When he had a good day with his "business" he would slip me a ten-dollar bill, a fortune in those days. If he had a bad day, he never showed it.

The rest of my mother's side of the family were Catholic, and they all worked in less dangerous and more genteel industries than my grandfather's. My Uncle Eugene worked as a truck driver. My Aunt Gertie was a seamstress and a proud union member who worked in clothing factories near to central Philadelphia. She also worked for a period of time in New York City for a factory that made bathing suits. But after a couple of years in NYC, she returned to her job and family in Philadelphia. My Grandmom Gottlieb was a stay-at-home mom and would often take care of me, my sister Bonnie, and my Aunt Rose Marie's daughter, Joann.

Before marrying my mother, my father, Edward Marion Gray had lived with his parents in Northeast Philadelphia, in my Grandmother and Grandfather Gray's row home. My Aunt Sandy, my father's younger sister lived there also.

My grandmother, Marie Gray, was lively and entertaining. She loved to dance and she was an engaging storyteller with an endless stock of anecdotes. A devoted grandmother, she would help my Dad and my Aunt Sandy with their kids while everyone else went to those Phillies baseball games. She never missed one of my Bishop Egan or Penn State home football games.

My Grandfather Gray had a job as an installation and repairman for the Philadelphia telephone company. Later he moved into management of the company. His job was safe from depressions and recessions, so although they lived modestly, my paternal grandparents were financially stable. Grandpop Gray also would go to all of my football games, so I had a lot of my family rooting me on when I took to the field. My Grandfather Gray very much liked to travel to the Jersey shore and would rent a home in Sea Isle City for a month during the Summer. My family and I would always come to visit for a long weekend, and for my sister Bonnie and I, it was always a highlight of our summer.

My Aunt Sandy was very pretty, smart, tall, and slim with curly-brown hair and dark eyes. She was closer in age to me than to my Dad, and I loved when she would let me tag along with her. Those early bonds strengthened with age. She came to my games

Family

when I played football in high school and college and her husband, my Uncle Bill Muir, would usually accompany her.

The Grays' row home was close to the Shibe Park baseball field where the Phillies played back in the days before Veterans Stadium was built. As I grew up and began to play Little League baseball, my Dad would take my Aunt Sandy and me to a couple of Phillies games a year. My desire to play big-league sports was honed there in the stands of Shibe Park. But my first tentative forays into sports were on the fields of Levittown…with my Dad still beside me.

My Blue-Collar Days

One of the reasons so many dads got involved in Little League in Levittown is because they could. The commute time from Levittown to jobs in the surrounding cities was not too painful. By car it was 30 to 60 minutes to Philadelphia or Camden, and just 20 minutes to Trenton. Train lines also linked Levittown northward into New York City; and south to Washington, D.C.

One of the easiest commutes of all was the one to the US Steel factory in Fairless Hills. The 2,500-acre facility eventually employed upwards of 10,000 people in Bucks County and, for an extremely short period of time, I was one of them.

I had turned out to be a pretty decent football player and I had a full athletic football scholarship to Penn State which took care of my tuition, room, and board. In the summer of 1969, after my freshman year at PSU, I earned my spending money by working in a steel factory. From that job, I learned that physically, I was not up to the task of working in a steel mill plant. During most of my time at the Fairless Hills Steel works, I was trying either to look busy or to hide from my foreman so that I would not become busy. Based on that summer job, I doubled down on my efforts to ensure a future as a lawyer, or a banker or some other profession where I could work in the air-conditioned comfort of an office instead of the hot and noisy floor of a factory. That insight was worth far more than the modest nest egg I accrued that summer.

The president of US Steel at that time was Ben Fairless. To provide housing for his employees, he took a cue from the Levitts. He contracted for more than 3,000 prefabricated homes to be built on a property adjacent to Levittown in Lower Bucks County in a

41

sub-division named Fairless Hills. Steel workers, who flocked to jobs at the Fairless Hills Steel Works, settled in both the new suburb of Fairless Hills and nearby Levittown. Homes were ready to be sold in both Levittown and Fairless Hills to house the steelworkers as they arrived in 1952 from Western Pennsylvania and other localities where steel was made.

The US Steel factory was situated on the industrial belt following the Delaware River that stretched from Trenton to Philadelphia. Barges and boats to and from US Steel made the Delaware a transportation link that rivaled the ever-growing network of roads.

Levittown commuters benefitted from the community's strategic setting at the confluence of four important arteries: US Route 1, US Route 13, the final eastern exit of the Pennsylvania Turnpike before it crosses over the Delaware River to New Jersey, and the road that would later become US Interstate 95. The well designed and maintained I-95 would eventually wind its way south from New England and through New York City, then down to Levittown, through Philadelphia and to Florida.

Besides US Steel, the other major employers in and around Levittown at the time were: Minnesota Manufacturing and Mining (3M), Kaiser Metal Products, and Rohm & Haas Corporation. Jointly, these four companies during that 1960s period employed about 60% of the labor force of Levittown and Lower Bucks County.

The typical family in Levittown was headed by a blue-collared or white-collared father who was the bread winner and a stay-at-home mother whose primary roles were domestic—at least until the children were in school. Many moms also worked part-time and some worked full-time to help with the family's expenses. My family met that description.

After his stint in World War II, my Dad was one of those veterans who could not resist Levittown's charms and baseball fields. He was a mechanic and had machinist skills. After leaving the Navy he worked at a series of blue-collar jobs around Levittown. He probably earned just enough money to cover our family's monthly expenses. I have no memory of lacking for anything important, but in retrospect, I'm convinced that my parents barely scraped by.

Frank Sinatra Chimes in on Education

To earn extra money, my mother was a singer in the bars and cabarets close to Levittown. She was very pretty with long brown hair, and she had a beautiful voice. I still have some of the 45-speed vinyl recordings and a tape that she made. She was popular on the stage of the bars and restaurants of Trenton, Philadelphia, and Lower Bucks County. Her proudest performance occurred when she invited Frank Sinatra, who was in the audience at one of her Trenton gigs, to sing a couple of songs with her. Together, they sang "Fly Me to the Moon," and "That's Life!" I wish I had been there for that performance, even though I was only in my teens. But that evening has become part of our family lore. If only it had been memorialized in a photograph.

My family, like other new homeowners throughout Levittown, were making memories and filling photo albums with Polaroids, the seemingly magic instant photography sweeping America. Their dream houses in the suburbs made perfect backdrops for the pictures that chronicled their children's milestones—first day of School, Holy Communion, graduations and holidays.

Each of the 41 neighborhoods had a name—Greenbrook, Stonybrook, Cobalt Ridge, etc., and the street names in each section started with the same letter of the alphabet as the neighborhood name. Garden Lane was where I lived in the Greenbrook section.

With the influx of young couples into Lower Bucks County in the early 1950s, the Levittown farm landscape changed quickly. In the early 1960s instead of potato fields we had French fries, courtesy of fast food restaurants such as McDonalds, Burger King, and Geno's—where in the summer of 1966, I worked flipping burgers right across the street from the Levittown Shop-A-Rama. Shopping centers with stores like Pomeroy's and Sears and Roebuck and Company were also sprouting. But the most important concern for the Levittown parents was the quality of the education for their baby boomer children.

Neither my father nor mother nor any of my relatives had ever attended college. When they graduated from high school, they entered the work force or got married to someone who could support them. Job satisfaction derived less from the day-to-day work and more from the size of the salary and generosity of the benefits. But in the hot post-war economy, the blue-collared sections of Levittown could see that those on the white-collared side had both good paychecks and rewarding careers.

All of my relatives tried to instill into me and to my sister, Bonnie, the importance of a good college education. So, their goal became mine. Before I had reached high school, I had set my sights on earning an athletic or academic scholarship to a well-respected university.

Competition was the Buzzword

With its cookie cutter houses, the community that the Levitts built was the picture of conformity. Separately, the home owners differentiated themselves from their neighbors by their accessories—the newest model car, a fancy grill on the patio, an elaborate backyard swing set.

The Levittown kids tended to distinguish themselves by their athletic prowess. Competition was the buzzword. Our competitive instincts were honed. We saw this quality with the new wave of children who would challenge one another and compete for positions on the football, baseball, basketball, soccer, and track teams of the Bishop Egan Catholic High School, which I attended, or in the three public high schools: Woodrow Wilson, Pennsbury, or Neshaminy, each of which educated high school students carved from the different geographical sections of Levittown.

Craig Eisenhart has particularly sharp memories of his school days because his father was a teacher in the Pennsbury School District. In the early days before school consolidation, the teachers at Woodrow Wilson High School, taught only students who were the residents of Bristol Township. "But the Pennsbury School District encompassed Falls, Fallsington, Lower Makefield and Yardley." Eisenhart recalled, "All of our schools were brand new. And in Levittown, we had an extra kick because of the new community that was being developed with 52,000 new people."

The shiny new buildings did not disguise how recently Levittown had been farmland, but that had its upside for Eisenhart. "I used to go to the YMCA there when they were building it," Eisenhart said. "I used to ride my bicycle, but there was an asparagus farm in that field. We had the best asparagus for like ten years, because somebody's farm in that field had been abandoned. And, there was another asparagus farm where Pennsbury High School now sits. We had the world's greatest asparagus because it was abandoned farmland. Mud everywhere though. I do remember my mother complaining about the mud."

Chapter 3

A Levittown Legacy and Me

When I tried out for the Bishop Egan freshman football team in the late summer of 1964, more than 100 students were vying for 40 slots. After a pep talk at the first session, the head coach of the freshman team introduced us to the quarter mile running track surrounding the football field and said one word: "Run!"

Panting and perspiring in the heat and humidity of a sultry August afternoon, we ran around the oval again and again and again. Each time we hoped it would be the last and that the coaches would whistle us into a huddle where the fun would finally start. But we just ran until our calves throbbed and our lungs burned. On the second day only 60-some boys showed up. Again, we ran and silently cursed our coaches. By the third day, the number of potential football players dwindled to a manageable group. The athletes who remained might not have been the most talented, but they had energy, stamina, passion, and love of the game. They were the ones who wanted to play at any cost.

My mother often said to me, "You can be anything you want to be, do anything you want to do, if you set your goal high and work hard enough to achieve it." I embraced this belief and I have lived by it. I consider it my Levittown Legacy. It has had a profound effect on me. My mother's words echoed throughout my life: as a young grade school athlete; as a college student-athlete on a football scholarship; as a PhD student earning a doctorate in Finance; as a business executive when I was a managing director of a Wall Street investment bank; as a college professor teaching Finance to 2,500 Penn State students per year; and as a husband and father of six wonderful children.

I think that most families in Levittown at that time had a similar sense that hard work and a will to succeed would make us competitive with America's best and brightest. (See Exhibit 1.) The Levittown Legacy was forged at the nexus of post-war optimism and unprecedented economic opportunity for the lower middle classes. The generation that had recently saved the world from tyranny was now building a super power nation.

In Levittown and the countless suburbs that followed, these young parents, workers, and returning veterans were also building a foundation for their children and grooming them to soar far beyond the economic, social and cultural heights they themselves had attained.

My early years in Levittown coincided with the establishment of NASA and the start of Project Mercury which aimed to put humans into space. NASA was an apt metaphor for my parents' generation. They were hopeful and confident. They had grand visions. And they launched their children like so many rockets from the shiny new schools and playing fields of suburbia. Academics at that time referred to the phenomenon as the "Revolution of Rising Expectations."

To me, it's the "Levittown Legacy," and I suspect that a version of it existed in every newly sprouting suburb of the 1950s and early 60s.

A competitive spirit was at the crux of the Levittown Legacy. Having moved out of a cramped row house in Philadelphia, I could sense the difference. All that was happening around me, made me believe that something exciting and exceptional was going on in Levittown. It was most apparent in athletics. I could see how intensely young athletes practiced and really worked to succeed. That competitive drive propelled many young Levittown athletes and teams to perform at extraordinarily high levels like the players on the 1960 American Little League All-Star team and also the football players from the four local high schools.

But the Legacy didn't just affect competition in sports. It also carried through to academics, producing young lawyers from Little League all-stars—Julian Kalkstein and Joe Fioravante, who eventually would defend their clients the way they had once defended a lead on the baseball diamond. The Levittown Legacy encouraged residents to compete and excel at all jobs

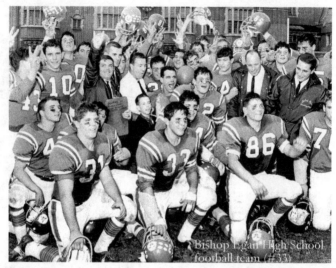

Bishop Egan High School football team (#33)

and all levels. Many of the young people who were nurtured in that early Levittown environment, went on to successful careers, great achievements, and interesting lives.

Sports figured prominently in the Levittown Legacy. By 1960, the town was packed with 11- and 12-year-old kids on the cusp of manhood. Among the boys, the better players would eventually play on the baseball, basketball, and football teams of the four high schools that served Levittown. When that cohort of young athletes reached 14- to 17-year-olds (1964-1967), they transferred their dominance to the football field. A look back at the football records of the three public high schools in Levittown—Woodrow Wilson, Pennsbury, and Neshaminy—along with the record of Bishop Egan High School, the Catholic school where I played baseball in 1964 and football from 1964-1967, reveals an extraordinary record as shown below in Exhibit 1.

Exhibit 1: Levittown High Schools
Football Records 1964-1967

Bishop Egan High School

'64	4-7	A very bleak year.
		Lost 0-21 to Neshaminy
'65	9-3	Philadelphia Catholic League Champs
		Lost 0-41 to Neshaminy
'66	12-1	Philadelphia City Champs
		Beat Neshaminy 41-0
'67	11-1	Philadelphia City Champs
		Beat Neshaminy 21-0
		and West Catholic 39-6

Total   36-12   Average=75% wins

Some great players from that era (my era) include: Pancho Micir, Jackie Lyons, Tom Duffy, Larry Marshall, Craig Kugler, Irv Whalen, Bill Bartholemew, Dan Morrin, Bobby Migliorino, Tony Petruccio, Tom Razzler, and Dave Frederick.

Woodrow Wilson High School

'64	8-2	Beaten only by Pennsbury and
		Neshaminy
'65	5-2-3	Beaten only by Egan and Neshaminy
'66	8-1-1	Beaten only by Egan
'67	3-7-1	Beaten by Egan and Neshaminy

Total 24-12-5 Average=67% wins (not counting ties)

Some of the great players that I can remember from Woodrow Wilson include: Rick Lewis, Gary Steele, Paul Horwatt, Jack Jacobik, Steve Schein, Vince Scarcella, Jack Watts, Rollie Clark, Rich Banyas, and Vince Thomson.

Neshaminy High School

'64	9-0-1	Lower Bucks County League Champ
'65	10-0-1	Lower Bucks County League Champ
'66	2-6-2	Coaching Change-lost to Egan 0-41, Wilson 0-20, Pennsbury 0-60
'67	3-7-0	Beaten by Egan 0-21

Total 24-13-4 Average=65% wins (not counting ties)

Some of the great players that I remember are Jim Colbert, Harry Schuh, Bill Brundzo, Jack Stricker, Michael Frederick, Fred Conger, Bob Baxter, Dale Forchetti, Pete Cordelli

Pennsbury High School

64	9-1	Lost to Neshaminy
65	6-2-1	Tied Wilson, Lost to Neshaminy
66	8-1-1	Lower Bucks County League Champ
67	8-2	Lower Bucks County League Champ

Total 31-6-2 Average=84% wins (not counting ties)

Great players include: Joe Fioravante, Bob Burkhart, Ed McManus, Jim Neeld, Vern Von Sydow, Doug Powell, Mike Yatsko, Bill Cooper, and Troy Vincent.

The aggregate win/loss totals for the four high school teams listed above for the four years from 1964-67 for all of the Lower Bucks County teams are:

Group Total: 115-43-11 Average: 73% wins (not counting ties)

The expected large sample win/loss average for the four Levittown High School teams should have been approximately 50%. Yet the actual average was 73 per cent. Did that inflated 73% win/loss average have anything to do with the existence of an active but barely understood Levittown Legacy, especially since the schools frequently played each other guaranteeing one loss per inter-Levittown team game? I would reply with a resounding "Yes."

I should also note that the quality of coaches was outstanding for these four teams during that time period. Dick Bedesem was the head coach of Bishop Egan High School for the four-year period which coincided with my playing days. He was a demanding and disciplined guy, but his love of the game and devotion to good sportsmanship won our respect and affection. In 1975, he left Egan to coach football at Villanova.

John Petercuskie, the head coach for Neshaminy during its heyday from 1960 to 1965, had a 59-1-5 record. He left Neshaminy in 1966 to become an assistant football coach at Princeton University. Coach Petercuskie recruited me to play football for Princeton. It was a beautiful medieval-style campus and its academic reputation was superb, but it was a little too close to home for me. Neshaminy's fortunes fell with the coaching change. Without Petercuskie, Neshaminy endured two losing seasons: in 1966 at 2-6-2 season; and in 1967 at 3-7-0 season.

Woodrow Wilson's head coach during this time period was Lou Sorrentino. My home in Levittown was in the Woodrow Wilson School District, and I knew Coach Sorrentino. I occasionally would see him when we were playing aggressive touch football games on the Woodrow Wilson football playing field, and he would try to encourage me to transfer from Bishop Egan to Woodrow Wilson. He seemed like a very good guy, and one of my best friends, Denny Glaum, played for Sorrentino. However, I decided to stay at Bishop Egan.

Pennsbury's head coach in the mid-60's was Erle Baugher. He had an outstanding coaching record with the highest winning percentage (84%) of the four schools and two Lower Bucks County Championships during the four-year period that I examined. Most of the Levittown American players went to Pennsbury High School, and a number of them contributed significantly to the success of the Pennsbury football program. Obviously, Pennsbury was a beneficiary of the Levittown Legacy.

When it comes to playing Little League baseball in Lower Bucks County, Dick Hart of Morrisville High School was the gold standard. Many people believed that Hart was the greatest all-around athlete to come out of Lower Bucks County. Hart was a baseball player, football player, and a track and field star. He turned down a football scholarship to Notre Dame (which I so much wanted!) and played guard for the Philadelphia Eagles until 1972, when he retired after a second knee surgery. He is remembered most for being the captain of and catcher for the 1955 Morrisville Little League Baseball team that won the World Championship five years before Levittown American reclaimed the honor for Bucks County.

The Levittown Legacy and Me

I believe that the Levittown Legacy was truly and deeply ingrained in me. My skills and interests shifted from baseball to football as I moved into high school. What did I have going for me in terms of physical prowess? I stood 5'11", weighed 204 lbs., and ran the 40-yard dash in 5.2 seconds. I was not really big, fast, or strong. In fact, I was barely adequate. But I was really *football smart*. From the glances of the opponent's offensive linemen, and the shifting of their weights and stances, I could sense out a play—a run or a pass—and a direction—run right or left—before it happened. I could sense the opponent's plays, and that is an important skill for a middle linebacker to have.

In fact, it used to drive my college football coach, Joe Paterno, crazy. If we were scrimmaging against the first team offense, I often yelled to a defensive end or to a fellow linebacker to watch for a particular pass or a direction of a run, or to pay attention to a hole in the line and I usually was proven right, and we, the defense, easily stopped the play. I understand that Joe thought that I was a wise guy, and he enjoyed yelling at me. He told me to play my position and to shut up. I never learned to keep my mouth shut, but I did whisper my calls when Coach Paterno was within hearing distance.

Playing smart helped me to compensate for my lack of speed. I attribute my slow 40-yard dash speed to my many years spent in the catcher position on the baseball diamond. I played catcher for my various teams in Little League and Connie Mack League and as a Freshman on Bishop Egan High School's varsity baseball team. Due to my constant ups-and-downs and the crouching on each pitch, my knees got battered and strained, and my running speed declined. I wanted it enough to sacrifice my knees. But being a catcher was a very physically demanding position.

I understand that with the better catcher's equipment of today, the young catcher's knees do not get as beaten up, as mine did in the 1960's.

The Big 33 Game and Joseph V. Paterno

With no speed or size to speak of, I got by with my ability to read an offense and an enormous will to win. I played inside linebacker at Bishop Egan. Larry Marshall, Craig Kugler and I were co-captains of that 1967 Egan team that won the Philadelphia city championship. Marshall and I also played in the 1968 Pennsylvania Big 33 game in Hershey, Pennsylvania, where the Eastern PA All Stars (Philadelphia and us) challenged the Western PA All Stars (Pittsburgh and them).

The Pennsylvania Big 33 game gave high school senior football stars a venue where they could show their talents to prospective coaches or to the teams they had committed to, prior to their attending a university or college as a freshman in the Fall. Sometimes an undrafted Big 33 player will have a good showing in the game and that player may receive a scholarship offer on the spot. Or at least, he may get the encouragement from a scout to try to walk-on or to at least get a try-out for a college.

My Big 33 teammates elected me to be the defensive captain of the Eastern PA team.

Our coaches were brilliant. They designed a defense that I really liked, that protected the middle linebacker—that was me. It was similar to a box-and-one basketball defense with me being the one. My fellow defensive players each matched up across from an offensive lineman and when the ball was snapped by the center, my teammates would have first contact against the offensive blocker in front of them. For example, we played our nose-guard over their center, our other linebackers on both guards, our defensive tackles over offensive tackles, and defensive ends outside. Opposite me was nobody but the quarterback.

I moved in precision with the quarterback. I followed him from one sideline to the other, and when he handed the ball off, because I often would be untouched, I would make most (25 to 30) of the Big 33 game tackles. I also intercepted two passes in the game and caused a couple of fumbles. I was named Most Valuable Player of that game, and it was all because of that box and one defense. I loved that defense.

On August 11, 1968, we beat the West Team 7-6. I had already committed to Penn State. But I was thrilled to know that Penn State Football Coach, Joe Paterno, was at the game. He came into the locker room afterwards to congratulate me and to touch base with the other high school players there that had committed to Penn State. Coach Paterno was quoted in the August 12, 1968 *Bucks County Courier Times* article entitled "20,000 fans Agree Egan's Gray is Terrific" that was written by Dick Dougherty. Paterno's quote was "Gary Gray looked awful good out there. It's not so much his two interceptions, you fall into things like that. But he's making a lot of tackles. Of course, I'm interested in Gray because he's coming to Penn State. But he played a wonderful game and was at the right place at the right time."

That half century old article is enshrined in my scrapbook. The game was a pretty heady experience for an 18-year-old about to leave home for college.

Coming out of high school, I had been recruited pretty heavily and a number of colleges wanted me for my "smarts" as Coach Joe Paterno would put it, especially Ivy League schools like Princeton, Cornell, Dartmouth, Yale, and the University of Pennsylvania. I had solid SAT scores and the Ivy League schools gravitated to athletes who were also good students and liked the fact that a student could be both smart and a good athlete.

My family couldn't afford to take airplane flights and long trips for vacations. Prior to college recruiting, I had never before flown in an airplane, and I welcomed the weekly flights to visit a college. I started the college visitation process with an open mind. The universities paid my airfare to Michigan, Ohio State, Florida, Virginia, Virginia Tech, and Maryland. For a kid who had never been farther than Williamsport and the Jersey shore, I felt like a newly minted member of the jet set.

Franco Harris and the Immaculate Reception

Every weekend of my senior year in high school, from late fall and through early spring, I was making a college visit. I loved being courted by top-notch schools. On several of my recruiting visits, I was part of a group that included a running back from nearby central New Jersey. I spent a lot of time with him never guessing that he would become a lifelong good friend. His name is Franco Harris.

Franco came from a very large family. He had, in order of age, eight brothers and sisters and each of their first names ended with a vowel: Daniella, Mario, Franco, Marisa, Alvara, Luana, Piero, Guiseppe, and Michele. Franco's father, Cad, was a World War II veteran. During his service time in Italy, he fell in love with a beautiful Italian woman named Gina from the town of Pietrasanta. He married her and brought her back with him to the United States.

Franco was everything I was not—strongly built at 235 pounds and 6 foot 2 inches, and fast. He ran a 4.7 second 40-yard dash speed. And he had plenty of raw, natural talent. And I just wasn't interested in lifting barbells in the weight room.

Two of Franco's brothers later attended and played football for Penn State. Piero had some outstanding years there leading the Penn State defense and the nation with ten pass interceptions and was a first team All American safety in 1978.

Franco grew up in the town of Mount Holly which was a stone's throw away from the third Levittown (now Willingboro, NJ) in west central New Jersey, right across the Burlington Bristol Bridge and only fifteen miles away from Levittown, Pennsylvania. He also roomed with me during our first three years in college in 1968, 1969, and 1970.

Franco was the 13th player selected in the 1972 NFL draft. During his professional seasons he rushed for 12,120 yards and scored 100 touchdowns, 91 running and 9 by air. The Pittsburgh Steelers won 4 Super Bowls with Franco. In the 1975 game, he was voted Most Valuable Player, and he also played in the 1974, 1978 and 79 Super Bowls and he has the 4 Super Bowl Rings to prove it.

Franco and I had both graduated from Penn State in May of 1972. I went into finance in Philadelphia and Franco was drafted by the Pittsburgh Steelers, where he won the 1972 NFL Rookie of the Year award. Franco would come to the attention and awe of the sporting world as the hero of one of the most spectacular football plays in history. In fact, he became a Pro Football Hall of Fame Steelers running back for a career that took-off after the *Immaculate Reception.*

The Immaculate Reception happened on December 23, 1972, in Franco's rookie year in the NFL. I had graduated from Penn State in June, so it was my first year out of college. I was living in Boulder, Colorado, soaking in the beauty of the Rocky Mountains, and working as a stockbroker for Paine Webber in nearby Denver. I was also helping to coach the University

Gary Gray with Franco Harris
honoring the 1970-71 team at Beaver Stadium (ca. 2000)

of Colorado freshman football team as a volunteer
assistant, and I was pondering whether to return to
college for an advanced degree. I was thinking about
Law School at Denver University or an MBA at the
University of Colorado's Business School in Boulder.

I had gone into a bar in Boulder to watch the 1972
football playoff game between the Pittsburgh Steelers
and the Oakland Raiders. In a hard-fought game, the

Steelers were trailing 7-6 with a 4th and 10 on their own 40-yard line with only 22 seconds left in the game and with no time-outs remaining. There was little hope left for the Steelers. Pittsburgh's Quarterback Terry Bradshaw took a snap from his center, and he eluded a couple of blitzing Raiders to launch a long Hail Mary pass down the middle of the field. It was intended for halfback Frenchy Fuqua.

The jump ball was hotly contested by Fuqua and two or three Oakland Raiders and the collision of bodies jolted the football out of the scrum. It got propelled into the air in the direction of rookie player, Franco Harris, who was sprinting down field in an attempt to get into the action. Franco bent down and just before the football touched ground, he calmly scooped it up from below his knees and only inches above the turf. Franco then side-stepped a couple of surprised Raiders, and I screamed with glee in that Boulder bar as he crossed into the end zone with the game winning play that would become part of pro football lore.

I started yelling, "That's my roommate, that's my roommate!" The patrons at the bar thought I was crazy. But once I explained my relationship to Franco, people wanted to buy me a drink and congratulate me as if I had scored the touchdown myself. I obliged and it turned out to be a pretty great evening.

Out to Colorado and Bad Rad

The reason I was in Boulder, Colorado, on the evening of the Immaculate Reception is another tribute to the Levittown Legacy. The linebacker coach at Penn State during my freshman and sophomore years was Dan Radakovich, known affectionately as "Bad Rad." Dan was a great coach and developed some terrific linebackers at Penn State such as Dennis Onkotz and Jack Ham. In fact, it was during his tenure that Penn State became known as "Linebacker U." Both Ham and Onkotz were my teammates during my stint at Penn State and both were first-team All American linebackers under Rad. In 1970, the University of Colorado made Rad an offer that he couldn't refuse. It was to be the defensive coordinator for the team and it included a big bump in salary over what he was making at PSU.

In 1972, I had just graduated from Penn State with a degree in electrical engineering, and I did not have a game plan in place for the rest of my life. I packed up one of my family's cars and started cross country. No NFL team had drafted me because of my slow speed and small size. I was looking to travel a bit and found my way to Rad's home in Boulder. After spending a night with him and his wife, Nancy, I asked Rad if Colorado needed a freshman linebacker coach.

At that time, the NCAA forbid freshmen from playing varsity football, but they could play on freshmen football teams. Rad acquiesced and I moved out to Boulder and lived with him and Nancy, for a couple of months. I coached the freshman linebackers, but

I was also working as a stockbroker trainee for Paine, Webber, Jackson and Curtis in nearby Denver. That was also part of the Levittown Legacy package. If you weren't quite where you intended to be, you buckled down and made the most of whatever opportunity you could find. For me, the Paine Webber program would lead to a promising career switch.

Bad Rad would later go on to coach with the Pittsburgh Steelers and the Los Angeles Rams. Rad won two Super Bowl rings with the Pittsburgh Steelers in 1974 and 1975—he was a tremendous linebacker coach with great technical defensive knowledge.

As for me, I worked with Paine Webber in Denver for about a year in the stock brokerage area. Remembering my fleeting experience at US Steel, I decided to apply to either a business school or a law school. I moved back to Penn State and enrolled in its MBA Program. I talked with Joe Paterno about becoming a graduate assistant football coach. He liked the idea. I was supported by Joe, and the Athletic Department hired me, paid my tuition and gave me a modest stipend. I enrolled in the Penn State MBA program, and I helped to coach Penn State linebackers.

Joining me in an advanced graduate degree program was one of my Penn State teammates, Frank Ahrenhold. He had played a season with the Steelers before likewise opting for an advanced degree at PSU and a career in business. We cemented a lifelong friendship in those years that continued into the next generation. My oldest son, David, who along with his younger brother, John,

Gary Gray coaching alongside Joe Paterno

played varsity soccer at Penn State, and remains a close friend of Rachel Ahrenhold, who lettered in swimming at Penn State. After getting my MBA, I continued to live close to the Penn State campus, and I eventually received a doctoral degree in Finance.

While I was taking academic credits toward my MBA and PhD, I was also working for a couple of New York-based investment banks. I climbed to a Senior Vice President for E.F. Hutton. After Hutton had financial problems and was acquired by Lehman Brothers, I became a Managing Director at Lehman. My specialty was municipal finance—Issuing bonds for cities, states, and school districts to build schools, sewage systems, airports, roads, and other municipal projects.

Municipal finance involved a lot of travel across the country to meet and greet with clients or potential clients. To be good at municipal finance, as opposed to corporate finance, it was not all that important for me to work out of a New York City office. So much of my work could be done from State College. However, I did have an office in Philadelphia and a small one in the New York City World Trade Center.

I would make the 240-mile New York City car ride, now on a recently completed Interstate I-80. It was an easy drive from State College, PA to report to my New York office, usually on a-couple of times-a-month basis. My office was very high up the North Tower of the World Trade Center with a very good view of Upper Manhattan. Unfortunately, due to 9/11, that office is no longer.

Sometimes I flew to meetings leaving directly from the University Park Airport. In those days, I knew some of the pilots. Due to my frequent flying, I believe that I must have been one of Allegheny Airlines better customers. At other times, I flew myself.

In my spare time, I had earned a pilot's license and I had bought a one-eighth (12.5%) ownership share in a four-seat Piper Cherokee 180 airplane. My wife, Katie O'Toole, also got the flying bug and she received her pilot's license shortly after I had received mine. In Katie's earlier days as an undergrad at Penn State, she was a member of its sky-diving team and she had racked up over 140 jumps.

So, if I wanted to get into New York I would fly the Cherokee 180 into and out of New Jersey's Teterboro

Airport, right across the river from New York City. I would train or cab or bus it into New York City from there. I also would fly my plane to meet with clients in smaller towns that were less accessible by car. A small private airplane makes it a lot easier to get to out of the way destinations. In fact, Katie and I used our Cherokee 180 to fly Kate's mother and father to Teterboro and then take a cab into New York City for lunch.

As an investment banker, I was pretty well compensated. Most PhD academic candidates were on a tight budget, and that could force them to choose between having a few drinks or eating a nutritious meal. When I think back to that era, it's apparent to me that I had it pretty good.

Also, as an investment banker I was lucky to have friends whom I have grown older with and whom I could rely on if I ever had troubles, and vice versa: David Seltzer, John Foote, Scott Perper, Rusty Lewis, David Eckhart, Pat Cusatis, and Mark Hattier.

But my good luck wasn't limitless. All three investment banking firms that I had worked for over the years—Paine

Webber, E.F. Hutton, and Lehman Brothers—all ended in bankruptcy or forced mergers or were taken over by another investment or a commercial bank. It was an era when investment and commercial banks had borrowed too much debt and had not issued enough equity. This time the government refused to bail them out.

Investment banks were highly leveraged, meaning that they had a large amount of debt (borrowings) and a very small amount of equity (ownership). During this time period—the middle to late 1970s, the typical Wall Street investment bank had on its financial statements in various forms, debt instruments totaling 90% to 95% of their balance sheet, with only 5% to 10% remaining in equity—ownership.

It is important for a risky business, such as investment banking and the primary financial markets, to have a larger percentage of equity to cushion any mistakes that might be made in the way of asset values declining, or some unexplained financial crisis that catches everyone by surprise.

Paine Webber, Lehman Brothers, and E.F. Hutton were all caught with their pants down as the value of the assets that they were financing with all of these borrowed funds, plummeted until losses exceeded the firm's equity. When that happens, the bank is technically bankrupt with its liabilities greater than its assets plus their equity. That is when the government steps in and closes down the bank.

Another 5-Star Recruit Comes to PSU

In 1967-68, long before earning his four Super Bowl rings and his induction into the Pro Football Hall of Fame, Franco was just starting to win some renown. Franco was one of two five-star, can't miss fantastic running backs coming out of New Jersey high schools who joined me as freshmen at Penn State. The other was Lydell Mitchell, who was a break-away runner, similar to today's Saquon Barkley, with extremely strong legs, power, and hurtling ability.

Lydell had 1,567 rushing yards and 29 total touchdowns in 1971, our senior year at Penn State. And he had tremendous speed and acceleration. He was about my height and weight, and he probably was a bit faster than Franco. He had an NFL's running back physique. Lydell was a first team All American halfback and was drafted in the second round by the Baltimore Colts in the 1972 draft. He was a Pro Bowl selection a couple of times and led the entire NFL in

Franco Harris, Gary Gray, Joe Paterno, Lydell Mitchell, and Jack Ham, after an event

pass receptions in 1974 and 1977. His total rushing yards over his career tallied 6,534 in the NFL. And he was and still is a good friend.

Graduating from high school, I had winnowed down my college choices and I became really interested in three big-time universities: Michigan, which I had visited and enjoyed my weekend stay; Notre Dame University, which did not offer me a scholarship despite my roots in a Catholic high school, (and I am still disappointed by their lack of interest); and Penn State in central Pennsylvania. From a distance standpoint, Penn State was my Goldilocks choice. It was just under 4 hours by car from Levittown—close enough for my family to come to games, but far enough away to give me some independence. Penn State had a spectacular campus, and it just felt comfortable to me. It had a relatively dynamic new head coach, Joe Paterno, who for almost two decades had been Penn State's offensive coordinator. Franco, Lydell and I were part of Paterno's second recruiting class, and it was a strong one. Also, Penn State gave off a tremendous vibe that a high school teenager could feel. I am sure that Franco and Lydell had also felt it. That's one of the reasons why they committed to Penn State.

Penn State Comes a Calling!

Franco was on another Penn State visit with me. That's when we really started to get to know each other, and we had a great weekend together. Penn State and State College looked promising. I really liked the campus and we went to a number of fraternity parties on Friday and Saturday night. And the feel of the campus, and the partyers and fraternity members were chanting "Choose Penn State."

One day in the early Spring, Franco called me at my home in Levittown and told me that he had committed to Penn State. Lydell also accepted a Penn State scholarship offer. The next day, Penn State Quarterback Coach, George Welsh, who was responsible for recruiting the Philadelphia area for Penn State, called and officially offered me a full scholarship. I accepted. The downside to that acceptance was that once you've committed, nobody was going to finance or take me on any more campus trips to show me his or her University. So, my flying career had quickly come to a stop.

In August 1968, when we freshmen players first reported to Penn State for pre-season football practice, we were housed in a dorm area in the central part of campus and we were temporarily paired up with teammates. My roommate was Charlie Zapiec, who was a sophomore offensive lineman later to move over to defense and become a linebacker. Charlie had played football for LaSalle High School and came from Philadelphia. We had played against each other in the Philadelphia Catholic League, and LaSalle gave us the one loss that Bishop Egan suffered in 1966. That loss still hurts. However, Bishop Egan still won the City Championship that year.

When I had made my first recruiting visit to Penn State, I had stayed with Charlie and his roommate, Jack Ham. They shared a dorm room during their freshman year. I had talked with Franco Harris about rooming with him on some of our recruiting trips together, and we thought we would make good roommates.

That was the beginning of the three-year period during which Franco and I shared Room A-30 Hamilton Hall in the West Halls dorm area. It was conveniently located for me near to the electrical engineering (EE was my undergraduate major) building. It was a ground floor dorm room and the window opened up onto the Phi Gam parking lot. We kept it year-round for three years. We never had to pack up our belongings or relinquish the control of our room for three years. I am sure that Coach Paterno and Coach Jim O'Hora, our defensive line coach, who also was active in making sure that the players were adequately housed and fed, arranged that setup.

In the early years that Franco and I lived in West Halls, there was a pretty co-ed that I had gotten to know through hanging out in the Commons area with her and her friends. Her name was Dana Dokmanovich and she had a slim 5'7" build, long black hair, and a feisty sense of humor. She had a great focus and determination. She was not afraid to speak out and to take risks. I had chatted her up in the dining hall and sometimes we would eat together. On one of those days I introduced her to Franco, who had joined us for lunch. Soon they became an item. Then a very serious item. They have now been married for more than 40 years. I guess that relationship has worked out pretty well.

We know how Penn State football worked out spectacularly well for first round draft choices and all-Pros, Franco and Lydell. How did Penn State football work out for me?

Under NCAA rules, freshmen were not eligible to play varsity football in 1968. Our freshman team played and won both of our contests against two other freshman teams that we played that season.

Penn State's Varsity football team was 12-0 in 1968, my freshman year. We won the Orange Bowl beating Kansas 15-14, and we were ranked number two in the country. We went 12-0 again in 1969, were ranked number two in the country, and again won the Orange Bowl, beating Missouri 10-3.

Dousing Joe Paterno after the Orange Bowl win in 1969
AP Wirephoto

American linebacker, Dennis Onkotz, (*Backer* linebacker was the term we used), and Jim Kates (known as the *Mike* linebacker—PSU term). Both Kates and Onkotz were seniors and starting inside linebackers in our 4-4-3 defense. The Mike linebacker often shifted to become a down lineman and the Mike played over the opponent's center or guard when we wanted to show a 5-3-3 defense.

In my junior year in 1970, I started at inside Mike linebacker and led the team in tackles with 96, which was pretty good since the Backer linebacker that year in Penn State's 4-4-3 defense was Jack Ham. In 1970, Jack was a first-team unanimous All-American and he later became an all-Pro linebacker for the Pittsburgh Steelers. In 1971, my senior year and second year as a starter, I led the team in both tackles--115, and in interceptions with five. I was a first-team Academic All-American linebacker and first team All-East linebacker—Not too shabby for a small, short, slow football player with bad knees that didn't have an NFL physique. The Levittown Legacy compensated for my physical shortcomings.

GOVERNOR SHAFER is drenched in a shower by victorious Penn State football players at the Orange Bowl in Miami. Teammates are (from left) Lydell Mitchell, Mike Cooper, John Booth, Mike Botts and Gary Gray. (Stories and more pictures on pages 25, 26 and 27.)

Gary Gray in action, number 30

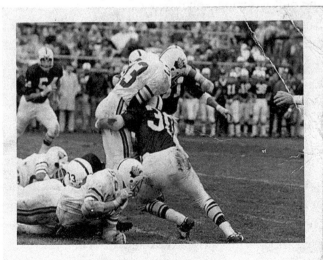

Chapter 4

1960's: Segregation, Vietnam
and the Counterculture

Memory being the imperfect storage unit that it is, I may have the tendency to idealize the Levittown of my childhood as being similar to the fictional suburban town where the Cleaver brothers in the 1960s got into and out of scrapes each week on "Leave it to Beaver." But from the moment the Levitts broke ground to build their development, there were dark undercurrents that would boil up in the coming decade, not just in Levittown, but nationally and around the world. As noted earlier, segregation was built by Levitt into the foundation of Levittown.

Levitt maintained that his exclusionary policy was simply a business decision. White families, he said, did not want to live next door to black families. In his first Long Island development, one that preceded the New York Levittown, Levitt refused to sell to Jews even though he himself was Jewish. The New York

Levittown and the Bucks County Levittown ultimately welcomed Jewish home buyers, but they kept and codified the ban on non-Caucasians known as the Levitt Rules.

In August of 1957, an African-American family— the Myers, moved into the Dogwood section of Levittown after buying a home directly from the previous owner. It was a flagrant violation of the Levitt Rules. The neighborhood took notice. Each night for two weeks after the Myers moved in, the protestors— angry mobs consisting mostly of young white men, gathered outside the Myers' home on Deepgreen Lane. They shouted, and taunted the family and threw rocks through windows, all while singing the National Anthem. Still, the family matriarch, Daisy Myers, refused to leave. The Pennsylvania National Guard was activated and helped to end the protests. With the National Guard protecting the Myers, the rock throwing incidents dwindled. Eventually, the protesters moved on, and Mrs. Myers was later labelled the "Rosa Parks of Levittown."

Both the National Association for the Advancement of Colored People (NAACP) and the American Civil Liberties Union (ACLU) fought Levitt's segregationist policy. The Federal Housing Administration (FHA) threatened to withhold mortgages on Levitt's next development which was underway in Willingboro Township in New Jersey. But Levitt would not back down until his ban was challenged successfully in court.

The plaintiff who forced an end to the Levitt Rules was W.R. James, an African American officer in the US Army's Criminal Investigation Division who was stationed at Fort Dix, near to the New Jersey Levittown. Applications for home ownership had to be made in person at the sales office, so when James appeared at the office to make a down payment, he was abruptly turned away. He sued, and his discrimination case went all the way to the New Jersey Supreme Court which upheld a lower court ruling in favor of James and the integration of Levittown. James died in 2016, but he lived to see one of the elementary schools in Willingboro Township, New Jersey named for him.

On February 1, 1960, the first *integration sit-in* occurred when a group of four black college students launched protests against racial segregation at a "Whites Only" lunch counter of a Woolworth store in Greensboro, North Carolina. The students were denied service but they refused to leave. They were joined by more students and the protests spread through the southern United States.

Those early years of resistance to integration had a profound impact on the Pennsylvania Levittown. I have no personal memories of the civil rights battles fought by Myers or James. Nor do I remember knowing about the *Levitt Rules*, at least not until the subsequent racial protests in Levittown were highlighted on television and reported in newspapers across the United States. In retrospect, I now see why I grew up in an unnaturally white community with little or no African-American, Asian, or Hispanic influence.

That would begin to change with the passage of the 1964 Civil Rights Act and the ongoing Civil Rights campaign for equality and freedom and opportunity for all, regardless of skin color. But those changes came slowly and too late for me to have the advantage of diversity in my upbringing. The racial makeup of my Catholic grade school and high school and my sports teams largely reflected the whiteness of Levittown.

Even now, the Pennsylvania Levittown is not what might be called ethnically diverse. According to the 2010 census, residents were 87.7% White, 5.1% Latino, 3.6% African American, 1.7% Asian, and 1.9% other. The needle has moved slightly in the right direction but it hasn't moved too far beyond when Levittown was governed by Levitt's Rules.

What Are the Levitt Rules?

As was the case with civil rights, I was barely conscious at age 10 of the social issues and events that simmered just below the surface in Levittown and the rest of the country in 1960. In 1958, Betty Friedan famously surveyed her Smith College all-female classmates at their 15th class reunion. Their collective restlessness and unhappiness in the roles of suburban housewives became the basis for her manifesto, *The Feminine Mystique*, which is widely credited with launching the second wave of Feminism—the first being the Suffragist Movement that resulted in women's right to vote.

But if the women of early Levittown were unhappy in their proscribed roles as mothers and housewives, they didn't share their resentments with their children. In memory, at least, the moms were cheerful supporters of their athletic sons—moving dinner time to accommodate practices, baking cookies for the team, cheering the players on, and encouraging their daughters to do likewise.

The women and girls of Levittown turned out enthusiastically to support their sons, brothers and friends, during the quest for gold for the Little League World Championship. The girls formed their own cheerleading squad. It included six 12-year-old girls: Marion Amoroso, Louise Bellavita, Pat Reilly, Jody Gervasi, Kathy Bellavita, and Eileen Kauffman.

No other Little League tournament baseball team had ever before brought a group of cheerleaders to the tournament.

The Levittown American team, needless to say, was thrilled to have a squad of attractive, agile girls as their boosters. And the girls were pleased to have a somewhat official function in Levittown American's march to Williamsport. They received a designated spot on the field or in the stands, and with their routines and cheers carved out their own role that extended beyond a support system for the boys. It was ground-breaking and might have been sufficient liberation for the young women of Levittown in 1960.

Like most 10 years-old at the time, I was oblivious to the political maelstrom of the era. We were vaguely aware of the Cold War mentality gripping the country.

But my impression of the Soviet Union was based mainly on the cartoon spies, Boris Badanov and Natasha. They were perpetually thwarted in their efforts to upend the Americans by Rocky, the Flying Squirrel, and his moose sidekick, Bullwinkle. Within a couple of years, the threat from the "Reds" would hit home during the Cuban missile crisis. Suddenly, black and yellow signs with icons relating to radioactivity were displayed on buildings to direct us to the "Fallout Shelter in Basement." We regularly took part in school fire drills and other safety precautions that we practiced for in the event of an atomic attack.

The sole political event that I can truly remember from 1960 was John F. Kennedy's campaign stop at the Levittown Shopping Center. In late October he was drumming up votes from union workers at US Steel and other factories where the laborers tended to vote Democratic.

Just weeks before his election on November 8, Kennedy received an enthusiastic welcome in Levittown. He played well to this crowd. With his youth, vigor, athleticism, and hopeful vision, he seemed to be a reflection of them. During the Soviet blockade that prompted a US-led airlift of supplies into Berlin in 1961, Kennedy would famously declare, "Ich bin ein Berliner." But on that autumn day in 1960 at the Levittown Shopping Center, he seemed to be saying, "I am a Levittowner!"

Nobody cheered him more heartily that day than Levittown's Catholic community. Only one other Catholic in US history had ever won a major party nomination. In the 1928 election, the Democratic Governor of New York, Alfred E. Smith, lost badly (444 electoral votes to 87) to Republican Herbert Hoover. By contrast, Kennedy seemed to be a viable candidate, and plenty of Catholic moms and dads like mine, made sure their children were at the shopping center that day to see history in the making.

At Saint Michael's Catholic Grade School and probably at countless other parishes around the country, priests added prayers for JFK's victory in their sermons, and not so subtly, they exhorted our parents to defy any separation of church and state and do their Catholic duty by sending Kennedy to the White House.

On September 26, Nixon and Kennedy debated on television, and many observers believe that Kennedy won the 1960 Presidential election based on his performance in that debate. Kennedy appeared on television as young, strong and vibrant. Vice President Nixon appeared older and in need of a shave compared to the bright-faced Kennedy, who was only four years younger than Nixon.

Soon after Kennedy's win by a razor-thin margin, a framed copy of his official portrait was hung on our dining room wall, right next to a gilt-edged picture of the Sacred Heart of Jesus.

After Kennedy was elected, almost none of us was paying attention to the conflicts of the world in the early months of the new President's administration. Few eyebrows were raised when he authorized the sending of additional Special Forces and other "advisors" to a place I had barely heard of–Vietnam.

Many boys who played Little League baseball

throughout Levittown and Bucks County would go to Vietnam. Some would lose limbs and lives on the battlefield. That story has been told in depth by my friend from Fairless Hills and a Vietnam veteran, Terry Nau, in his book, *We Walked Right Into It: Pennsbury High and the Vietnam War*. Pennsbury lost 15 of its former students in the war. Nau noted that Kennedy raised the number of Americans deployed to Vietnam from 900 during the Eisenhower Administration to 16,300 in 1963 when Kennedy was assassinated. U.S. troop levels in Vietnam, then under President Lyndon B. Johnson, would ultimately reach more than a half million in 1968.

On the drive up to Williamsport in 1960, the car radio most likely would have been serenading my Dad, Uncle Leon and me with Elvis Presley's number 1 hit, "It's Now or Never," an apt description for the outcome of the Little League tournament. Also, we must have heard Brian Hylan singing, "Itsy Bitsy, Teenie Winnie, Yellow Polkadot Bikini," that was released in June, and the Drifters "Save the Last Dance for Me." But the song that I remember all the girls singing that year was a 1958 hit from the Kingston Trio titled, "Where Have All the Flowers Gone?" They probably enjoyed the catchy folk melody, and repetitive lyrics made it easy to remember. I doubt we kids caught its anti-war, anti-establishment message, and in retrospect, our young parents may not have either—even though we were already—blindly, naively—on the path to what would become the longest war in American history. It bears mentioning here because some of the boys on Levittown American would be in Vietnam before the decade ended.

Where Have All the Flowers Gone?

I remember how my seventh-grade cohorts and I cried when President Kennedy's assassination was announced on Friday afternoon, November 22, 1963 over the Saint Michael's grade school's loud speaker system. In less than three years, Kennedy had become a revered figure in our part of the country, a charismatic man, eloquent speaker, husband of a beautiful wife, and father of two precocious children. His brief Presidency had transformed the United States. We treated his assassination like a death in our own family.

As we learned throughout that horrid weekend, that Kennedy was assassinated while riding in a motorcade through Dealey Plaza in downtown Dallas. He was prepping for a re-election run in 1964, and he had travelled through and had spoken to crowds in nine different states in less than a week. JFK was assassinated by Lee Harvey Oswald, who was quickly arrested. Two days later, on Sunday morning while most of America was tending to church duties, Oswald was shot and murdered at close range in the Dallas jail by a night club owner, Jack Ruby. The assassination was captured live, on television, and added to the brutality and horror of a weekend that changed America forever.

Kennedy's successor, Vice President Lyndon Johnson, quietly advocated a growth of troop levels in Vietnam. After his landslide re-election victory in 1964, Johnson felt confident enough to expand troop levels in the war zone.

Vietnam was considered a *conflict* rather than a war. In 1941, the US declared war on Japan and Germany, but never did it declare war on North Korea or North Vietnam, even after sending hundreds of thousands of troops to Vietnam — a number of them who had been playing baseball earlier on Levittown's Little League baseball fields in 1960.

Three of the Levittown American players on the 1960 All-Star team would end up fighting in the Vietnam War. Jim Grauel graduated from Pennsbury in 1965 and went on active duty in the Marines before the month of June had ended. Joe Mormello joined the Army after graduating from Rider College in 1969 and fought as an airborne infantry soldier. Rodger Barto joined the Air Force and saw action on several fronts.

Less than a decade after they were honored in 1960 by a cheering crowd of 25,000 people as they paraded through Levittown with their World Championship trophy, these three veterans would come home to the jeers of anti-war protestors. They would quietly put away their military uniforms and decades would pass before their valor on the battlefield would be recognized with the same respect given them for their heroics on the Little League field.

Ultimately, the Vietnam War would claim over 58,000 American lives.

I sometimes feel survivor's guilt that many of my friends and teammates served our country in the Vietnam War, while I did not. I took the S-2 college student exemption from 1968, my freshman year at Penn State, and that exemption ran out until after

I graduated in June 1972. In 1973, I failed my draft physical due to my battered catcher's knees. I had never thought that I would be grateful for those knee injuries. At the time, I felt lucky. With some perspective, however, as I came to appreciate the physical and emotional pain that scarred so many in my Levittown cohort, I understand and appreciate the enormous sacrifice of those that did serve.

The War lasted until the fall of Saigon on April 30, 1975. The official count included 58,318 US soldiers killed and 303,644 wounded. Over a million North Vietnamese and Viet Cong were killed and over 600,000 were wounded. For what?

In the late 1960s, we boys/men of 18 and older became familiar with, and scarred by and scared by several terms that were being used in the newspapers of the day.

Conscription — technically the formal name for the "Draft," it is the compulsory enlistment of people in a military service. The Selective Service Act of 1917 authorized the US Federal Government to raise a national army for service in World War I through conscription. It is designed to ensure that men of a certain age would serve their country for a number of years on active military duty and then transfer to reserve forces, or retire from service completely. In 1964 the United States drafted 112,368 men. In 1965 there were 230,991 men drafted and in 1968, 382,010 men were drafted.

The US ended the Draft in 1973 and converted to an all-volunteer military force. However, Federal law still requires young men between the ages of 18 and 25 to register with the Selective Services. Only men 20 years old and over were draft eligible.

The Draft — These two words struck fear into the hearts and minds of most males between the draft ages of 18 and 26 in the late 1960s. The draft was so unpopular politically that President Nixon invoked a lottery system that debuted on December 1, 1969. The bizarre event was conducted with 366 blue plastic ping-pong type balls containing the 365 birth dates in 1969, and one for the February 29 to account for leap year birth dates.

Like a huckster at a carnival, Congressman Alexander Pirnie of New York drew the clear blue plastic capsules. The balls were selected from a large glass container. Their selection was covered by the press and at the time it was also broadcast on television. I have bad memories from long ago listening to a radio broadcast of the draft and watching it on CBS News, rooting that my draft number would be 365. The government entity that supervised the Lottery was called the US Selective Service.

The order of call for induction during calendar year 1970, and for male US residents with a birth date between January 1, 1944 and December 1, 1950. The final Draft took place on March 12, 1975 for year of birth of 1956.

My birth date is April 18, 1950. Draft number N69 gave the results of the Draft Lottery held on December 1, 1969, for men born from 1944 through 1950. My birth date in that draft number was the 90th number called. From this drafted group in 1969, the highest lottery number that would be called by the draft for active service in 1969, was number 195 — well above my number 90. As I was recently discussing the draft with Steve Amoroso, he mentioned that his birth date lottery number came up last that year, the 365th group to be called. Now how lucky is Steve?

The Draft continued and the men drafted by the Selective Service during this time period had been born during the years from 1944 through 1953. The Draft was not popular, especially among teenage blue-collar worker types. It also forced many male teenagers, who after high school otherwise would have gone immediately into the work force, to enroll in college and spend lots of money for tuition and to get the S-2 exemption.

Counterculture—The blowback from the Vietnam War would ultimately lead to be one of the most tumultuous and consequential decades in US history. Within 5 years of Levittown's World Championship victory, the idyllic suburb would be rocked by the social changes sweeping across America. Long-haired, bearded, and beaded protestors would take to the streets to vocally reject the values of their parents. Flower Power would become the rage. *Sex, Drugs, and Rock and Roll* would be the mantra. Hippies and other protesters would demand civil rights for blacks, equal rights for women, and economic security for the poor.

But Levittown was no Haight Asbury, and in 1960, Flower Power, Hippies, and mind-altering drugs were in the alternate universe at the other end of the decade. Although its large blue-collar population tilted Levittown toward the Democrats, in 1960 it was a fairly conservative community of World War II and Korean War military veterans and their families. We held hometown parades on Memorial Day. We went to church on Sundays. Our dads drank beer, listened to baseball games on the radio, and washed their cars in the driveway. Our moms drank high balls and danced the Twist at neighborhood parties as Chubby Checkers serenaded them. But their children eventually rebelled.

By the mid-1960s, college campuses had become hubs of protest as American male collegiate students, who were most directly affected by the draft, rose up and demanded a withdrawal from the war in Vietnam, a desegregation of schools, and freedom of speech. Students questioned their country's political leadership and the role of American government institutions. A counterculture emerged that embraced illicit drugs and casual sex. Students for a Democratic Society (SDS) was created at the University of Michigan and first met in Ann Arbor. SDS soon became a radical student political organization and a blueprint for other colleges.

And, we boys who were 10, 11, and 12 in that summer of 1960? We played Little League baseball.

Chapter 5

The Quest for Williamsport and Local Games

The goal for each of the hundreds of thousands of young baseball players around the world, who participate in Little League baseball, is to become part of their local All-Star team. The Holy Grail for every Little League All-Star team is the World Series trophy.

In 1960, Levittown's prospects seemed unusually promising. The community teemed with the first wave of baby boomers, and neighborhood life revolved around the baseball playing fields. In Levittown there was no shortage of kids who could hit, pitch and field.

The All-Star Selection Process:

The 1960 regular season ended in mid-July for the majority of little leaguers in Levittown. Some families packed their cars and headed for New Jersey beaches or for visits with distant relatives. Released from the grind of practices and games, most small ballers were free to travel or to spend their time at swimming pools or on basketball courts. A lucky few, however, exchanged their summer vacations for a quest for glory.

"How did it impact my summer vacation?" Julian Kalkstein, one of the team's ace pitchers recalled many years later. "Baseball **WAS** my summer vacation."

Steve Amoroso was the son of one of the coaches, Gene Amoroso, and Steve pitched batting practice and played the field in the seemingly endless practices. He was a 10-year-old and he was prepping to try out for the 1961 team as an 11-year-old, so he tagged along with his dad to practices and games. He remembers the meetings of the head coaches from the six American Little League teams as they went through the process of choosing the all-star players. About 40 players tried out over a series of practices that stretched across a week. The sessions lasted about four hours a day, and each practice involved constant hitting and fielding.

The Amoroso's lived next door to the American League's baseball field. The coaches would caucus at their house and assess the players who were competing for 17 spots. Bill Dvorak was the head coach, and he had final say on who would be on the team. All the other regular season coaches had been invited to or had participated in the practices leading up to the final selection that would take place at the Amoroso home. Young Steve can remember his 10-year-old self, lingering among the gathered coaches as they analyzed and lobbied for one player or another. Finally, his father commanded, "Steve, Go to your bedroom!" And Amoroso knew that the final selections were about to be made.

Almost 60 years later, Craig Eisenhart still remembered how he felt when he was informed that he had made the team.

"Relieved," he said. "I remember the 1960 tryouts and being picked among the 14 players and three alternates. There was a lot of competition and at 11 years old it was difficult to handle."

Craig was one of four 11-year-olds to be selected, along with infielder/outfielder Gary Saft, infielder Chet Gardner, and catcher Brian Pennington. Four 11-year-olds is a big number on a 17-player roster. But those four players were expected to improve and mature, and they will form the foundation of the 1961 team, because they already have been there. The 1961 team should be pretty good.

Jim Grauel was another of the lucky ones who remembers getting the call. He had played first base and center field for Penn Fruit in the regular season. He didn't initially grasp the importance of being selected for the All-Star team. But his dad, a welder, understood. And his mom?

"My mom cried when she found out since she came to all of my games." That's when Grauel knew that making the All-Star team was a big deal.

The competition for a position was so intense that even some of the stand-out athletes were passed over. One that Eisenhart remembered was Bill Cooper.

"Cooper went on to become the Pennsbury High

School quarterback and later quarterbacked at Albright College." But there was no place for him on the American All-Star team.

"I was surprised that he didn't make the team," Eisenhart said.

The All-Star Positions Are Made

With the All-Star selections made, the coaches started the critical task of finding the right position for each player. The idea was to create a lineup where each player had the greatest chance of personal success while also putting the team in the best position to win the game. By necessity, the line-up was crafted quickly.

Kalkstein doesn't recall any frenzied moments associated with early practices. "The coaches did not necessarily give explicit advice," he said. "We practiced a lot. They let the team play. Sure, they set out the lineup and made tactical decisions, but it was with calm, without hurry and without any psychic weight on any of the team members."

The top two spots were "no-brainer" picks for pitchers, Kalkstein and Joe Mormello. It was not unusual for an All-Star team to have one dominant pitcher, but it was unbelievably lucky for a team to have two who were as gifted as Mormello and Kalkstein. Having two great pitchers allowed them to alternate on the mound, pitching every other game to abide by the regulations of the Little League All-Star tournament.

In the 1960 tournament, Mormello would strike out an amazing 89% of the players he faced and Kalkstein's strikeout percentage would be close behind. Neither would allow an opposing team to score more than four runs in a game, and between them they would record a total of two no-hit, five one-hit, and four two-hit games. Plus, they had good control of their pitches and did not give up many walks or hit many batters, both of which are just like giving up a single. Such pitchers' errors often hurts the team and results in runs for the opposing team.

Another bit of good news for the Levittown American All-Stars was that Mormello and Kalkstein, who both pitched right-handed, could hit as powerfully as they pitched. Kalkstein, a left-handed batter, would become the lead-off hitter in all the All-Star games and he would play third base when not pitching. When Mormello was not on the mound, he would play shortstop, and he would hit 10 home runs during the tournament.

Physically, Kalkstein and Mormello were an unlikely duo. Joe Mormello's height was 5-feet, 2-inches and he weighed 130 pounds and had a strong, compact, powerfully-built body waiting for his male growth spurt in height. Almost exclusively, he pitched an accurate and very scary high-speed fastball, and he would overpower the majority of the 126-opponent player at-bats who he would pitch against over the 13-game tournament.

Julian Kalkstein, who at 5-foot, 8-inches was a half foot taller than Mormello, and he had a long, lanky body that was perfect for his pitching repertoire and his high-kick form that he had adopted to mimic the high kick delivery of Warren Spahn, a 13-time major league all-star. Spahn was a left-handed pitcher for the Milwaukee Braves from the mid-forties through the mid-sixties, and was a Cy Young award winner. While Mormello had his overwhelming fastball to scare and push back the batters and get his strike outs, Kalkstein had a strong fast ball and some great curve balls and change ups, which often resulted in wild swings from the frustrated opposing batters.

Also known as "Smiley," Joe Fioravanti was left-handed and he seemed to have unflappable reserve on the field. That would serve him well later in life when he became a lawyer. He was a United States prosecutor in the FBI's ABSCAM investigation and the subsequent trial for bribery and corruption, which took down one Senator, six Congressman and a number of other corrupt officials.

"The two things that made us World Champions were superb pitching and an unbelievable adult commitment of time, energy and expertise," said Joe Fioravanti. All you really need in Little League are two strong pitchers. That is the rotation. We had two overwhelming pitchers. We had pitchers that were unhittable. One with guile, Jules Kalkstein, and one with just overpowering speed, Joe Mormello."

Supplementing the Mormello/Kalkstein pitching rotation was Tom "Tucker" Schwartz as a 12-year-old and Craig Eisenhart, who was an 11-year-old. Craig also was prepping for the 1961 All-Star team and pitched a lot of batting practices. They were the top pitchers for their respective regular season teams. As back-ups to the two stellar starting pitchers, Schwartz and Eisenhart wouldn't have much opportunity to display their pitching talent. But knowing they could be called upon for relief pitching surely gave an extra jolt of confidence to the coaches. Tucker started one game at pitcher when Mormello felt ill at game time. Eisenhart pitched to his teammates during many batting practices.

Schwartz rarely took the mound, but he would prove to be a solid pinch hitter. Tucker went on to be a dominant high school pitcher in Lower Bucks County. He pitched two one-hitters in his senior year, and he developed a devastating slider that was unhittable.

As for Eisenhart, when he wasn't playing the outfield, he was playing a piano. Throughout the tournament, he would occasionally tickle the ivories to help relax his teammates between games and he played a very important leadership role on the 1961 Levittown American All-Star team that would make it to the 1961 World Series.

With four strong pitchers, the next most important slot to fill was the catcher position. Levittown American was gifted in that department as well. Any Little League catcher (I know, I was one) would have had problems hanging onto Mormello's fastball or Kalkstein's curve. But Brian Pennington and Jim Fleming were the best catchers in the league. Both would prove to be a steady target behind the plate for Mormello and Kalkstein.

Pennington had a great arm for a catcher. He also pitched a couple of times during the regular season. Craig Eisenhart remembered being hit in the head by a pitch when Pennington was on the mound. And Craig still complained to me that, "It hurt."

The 1960 Levittown American Little League program which provided a recap of the quest, noted that "Fleming made the greatest play of the whole tournament. With a man on third and a wild pitch, Jim whirled and dove at the backstop. While lying on his back, he flipped the ball to Mormello, the pitcher, who was covering home just nipping the runner trying to score. Final score 3-2." That heroic play occurred in the final game for the State Championship.

Craig continued: "As far as when 11-year-old Pennington, whose nickname was Bunky, was in one of the seven tournament games that he caught, his steady target helped our pitchers develop confidence and control throughout the tournament. Bunky was a real holler guy and work horse, giving us a definite advantage for the next year's 1961 All-Star team behind the plate."

With the battery set, the rest of the line-up would now fall into place.

Chet Gardner was a rangy, strong first baseman who could also hit. In fact, he would end up with the team's second highest batting average over the term of the tournament. At second base was Rollie Clark. He wasn't very tall, but he was muscular and strong and added defensive strength at a key position. Rollie could speak Spanish which proved useful in Williamsport when the Levittown American players interacted with a team from Monterey, Mexico. Don Bickel played both third base and shortstop, alternating positions depending on who was on the mound. When Kalkstein pitched,

Mormello played shortstop and Don played third. When Mormello pitched, Kalkstein played third and Don shifted to shortstop. He was a versatile fielder who quickly would become one of the real bread-and-butter players of the team. Some of the parents and fans in the bleachers compared him to Marty Marion, who was known as "Mr. Shortstop" when he played for the St. Louis Cardinals in the 1940s, although the comparison to such an old-timer was probably lost on young Don.

The outfield likewise was made up of solid players with strong arms, good speed and great agility. Left fielder Mark Griffith had tremendous speed and specialized in the basket type catches that were becoming Roberto Clemente's signature move in Pittsburgh. In center field, Jim Grauel drew comparisons to Willie Mays with an arm like a rifle. Joe Fioravanti played right field with poise, confidence, and joy.

Gary Saft and Rodger Barto filled in where needed in both the infield and outfield. Their ability to play in multiple positions and their reliable batting cemented the sense that this team had the mettle to be champions. But for good measure, they had three alternate players, David Lenhart, Harry Cramer, and Chuck McCabe, who could be relied upon if one of the other players needed to be replaced for illness or a serious family conflict.

On the Practice Field

Julian Kalkstein later became a lawyer in a New

York City law firm. Certainly, as a lawyer, pitcher and world champion, he embodied the Levittown Legacy. His competitive instincts on the field carried over into the classroom and onto the court. After four years as an undergrad at Penn State and a stint at the Boston University School of Law, he went to work in criminal law in Brooklyn's District Attorney's Office for six years before moving into the appeals division of the Office of the Corporation Counsel for New York City.

"Levittown was a great place to grow up," he said. "It is hard to imagine now, but during the summer I would take off on my bike in the morning and come back in the early evening. No cell phones! My parents had no idea where I was! No one called home. I was either playing ball or at the pool. Looking back, Levittown was a combination of innocence and freedom. Some of my friends then, remain my closest friends to this day."

Like so many of the Levittown Baby Boomers, Kalkstein's youth was shaped by the easy access to sports, the friendships forged on athletic teams, and the work ethic modeled by industrious parents who saw an upwardly mobile future for their sons and daughters.

"I started playing baseball when I was eight-years old and I also played Pop Warner football. In junior high--soccer, baseball, wrestling; in high school—soccer and baseball. My father sold fabrics in New York City and my mother was a homemaker for me and my brother Josh, who taught me the game of baseball."

Among the athletes Kalkstein befriended in the

summer of '60 were boys who recently had played for his league rivals. But the players soon bonded over their shared goal.

"I do not recall much rivalry if at all," Kalkstein said. "Instead the team coalesced quickly into a working unit. I knew most of the players already. I knew Mark Griffth since I was five, as he lived on an adjoining street. I was friends with Joe Mormello and Joe Fioravanti. This was all occurring within a young, energetic community. Life was easy going. Life was on the neighborhood street or at the pool."

The Magnolia Hill Pool was the site of the Levittown American Little League home field. There was a popular fenced area with a concrete block wall. Craig Eisenhart remembers playing competitive stickball there and having a very good time at it--except for the summer of '60, when life was on the baseball diamond for both the All-Stars and their coaches.

Memories of Coaches and
Other Significant Contributors

Clearly, the time commitment to get Levittown American ready to play ball at a very high level was significant. Team fathers rescheduled their work time to be available to help at practices. Some of them essentially put in eight-hour baseball days to help with the team. Each of the men knew that this might be their son's chance to excel, to make a name for himself and his family at such a young age.

To lay the groundwork for a serious run on the Little League World Championship, Dvorak, Witt, Gardner, Amoroso and the parents pledged to devote the necessary time and energy to the quest. Jim Grauel remembers that the coaches often reminded the boys "what a win would mean for the team, family, community."

Most of the dads who volunteered with the team had also served in World War II where their hard work, sacrifice, and can-do spirit would mold them into what Tom Brokaw would later dub "the Greatest Generation." This group of men, who had recently helped a young nation to become a global power, now turned their attention to a smaller field of competition. And a young, upstart community was about to become the superpower of Little League baseball.

Head Coach Bill Dvorak worked full-time at US Steel, so he relied on other coaches and parents to help to make sure that the team had three practices a day. The first practice started at 7 AM before Dvorak went to work. An early afternoon practice was kept short (due to the heat) and was supervised by parents and coaches. The day wrapped up with a final session at 6 PM so that Dvorak could run it.

"The deportment and attitude of the coaches, to my mind, explains the success of the team," Kalkstein said. "The team had terrific talent. But it was the attitude, mind set and poise of William Dvorak and Roger Witt that made the team work."

The coaches struck a balance with their players.

They pushed them hard enough to draw out their best effort. They also understood that these were kids, 11- and 12-year-olds, who loved baseball as a game, not as a job.

"We were young and the coaches allowed us to have fun, enjoy practices, to be relaxed," Kalkstein said. "The team had a strong competitive spirit and character without needing to be prodded. What the coaches allowed was for the team to be at ease; they did not engage in significant discipline."

The three-a-day practices no doubt exasperated some of the parents. And as the team began its winning streak, there were growing pressures on the players to continue their high level of performance. But Kalkstein said the coaches shielded them from the worst of it.

"The outside anxiety, urgency and hysteria was not allowed to leak into the consciousness of the team's psyche," he said.

Many years later, Kalkstein ran into one of his old pitching coaches, Roger Witt, when the team was being inducted into the Bucks County Hall of Fame. "I literally had not seen him since the Little League summer of 1960. Bill Dvorak had passed away some time before. I recalled instantly Roger's ready smile, his ease, his poise. He was a kind man. He and Bill treated the team well. They were never frenetic; you never sensed the stress and strain I am sure they felt. As we climbed the ladder, they remained unruffled, imperturbable, and collected. Each game was simply the next game. I cannot emphasize this enough."

Although Kalkstein was chosen mainly for his pitching prowess, his more vivid memories were of batting practice. "Roger Witt probably ruined his arm throwing batting practice," he said. But in the process, Kalkstein's bat came to life in a way that it never had in the regular season.

"What happened to me was I got my *eye*," he said. "All these years later I can recall that during the tournament run to the World Series, I could *see* the ball as I had never seen it before. The ball came in big. When you *see* the ball, you can hit the ball. It really paid off for me."

The evidence of that pay-off is contained in a weathered gray briefcase that is crammed with old newspaper clippings, photographs, schedules, rosters and a booklet on rules and regulations. The briefcase belonged to Gene Amoroso, who was both a de-facto coach and the team scorekeeper. Fifty-eight years later, when I met with his son, Steve, loaned me the briefcase. I hungrily pored over its contents. Among its treasures? In red ink on a sheet of graph paper was a hand-written compilation of overall statistics for each player over the 13-game period. Kalkstein had a scorching batting average of .600. Mormello had a batting average of .400 and ten home runs. Other players who batted over .400 were Chet Gardner at .407, Joe Fioravanti at .434, and Don Bickel at .411.

Along with the briefcase, Steve Amoroso gave me details about the men who molded the 1960 team. In his own words with information about and descriptions of the contributors. He kindly did so in the paragraphs that follow.

Tom Diiorio was a coach and the team's purchasing agent. "He was one of many contributors who devoted an enormous amount of time to the Little League program. Mr. D was in a unique position because of his job was with Lower Bucks County or Falls Twp. sewer and water authority so he was always in the neighborhood and he could find some down time during the day to prepare the field and help with practices and equipment needs. He had a great sense of humor and was one of my parents' best friends and was very knowledgeable about baseball."

Another was Chet Gardner, Senior, whose son, Chet Junior, was one of the 11-year-old players on the team. "Chet Senior was a quiet man with a big presence always with a cigar in his mouth," Amoroso recalled. "Mr. G was employed at US Steel which gave him the ability to work a swing shift and be flexible to run practices during the day, which I believe was a big factor as the team was able to practice during the day and at night. He had a booming voice and when he spoke you listened."

Roger Witt, Coach. "His son Gary Witt was one of my best friends but Gary played in the Continental Baseball League, but his dad, Roger, stayed and managed in the American League for the next two years because he appreciated the talent that was in that league, and he believed he could be useful. Mr. Witt was a printer at the Trenton Times or the Trentonian… and he always ran the evening practices. The following year he managed the 1961 All Star team. He was a good hitting instructor and he helped me greatly during tryouts that year. Beside my Dad, Mr. W. was probably one of the foremost team spokesmen. He was a real salesman with a great personality and the gift for gab."

Naturally, there's a special place in Amorosos memory for his dad Gene, the team's scorekeeper/ Coach. "He was an insurance adjuster for Nationwide Insurance," Amoroso said. "He was the manager of Halperin in 1960 and became the American League President in 1961. He was a designated scorekeeper and coach for the All-Star team."

Little League tournament rules, specified that each team could officially have only one manager and two coaches, hence the scorekeeper title.

"My dad's main contribution to the 1960 team was to keep everyone loose. He always had a funny story or a way to keep everyone's spirits up. One of his famous tales had him skiing on one leg down the Himalayan Mountains after his plane crashed during World War II. Because our house was just down the street from the pool/baseball field, it was a gathering place for many team meetings and strategy sessions. My Mom always had the coffee pot going. My Dad coined the phrase '*All the way with Levittown A*' early in the tournament run."

Amoroso remembers head coach Bill Dvorak, "the glue that put and held this all together. Dvorak and his wife were godparents to the Amoroso's youngest daughter, Beth.

"They held a special place within our family" Amoroso said. "My dad and Mr. D, forged a friendship starting in 1958 when my dad became his assistant coach when he managed Watson and Schwartz. "Mr. D led them to consecutive league championships and was the logical choice to manage the All-Stars."

Dvorak commanded the respect from both adults and his players. "Everybody wanted to play for Mr. D and he always took time to talk with you especially about baseball," Amoroso said. "He personally took time to point out things I was doing wrong and praise what I was doing right, which he did for each and every one of his players. He was reserved and not one to seek out the spotlight but behind the scene he ran the show."

"As I step back these many years later," Amoroso added. "I can marvel at how cohesive and professionally run this coaching staff was especially at this level of competition. All the right pieces were there at the right time to guarantee success for this pool of talented players."

Amoroso said that Dvorak's competitive zeal never clouded his sense of fair play. One of Amoroso's lasting memories of Dvorak was an incident that happened in the fall of 1960.

"Regarding Mr. D, I have a personal story that sheds light on his character and his perception of how he wanted to be observed as a person, and that his success as manager of a little league world championship team would not affect how he made life decisions. In the fall of 1960, the biggest Pop Warner football game of the year was between Amvets, the 2-time and reigning league champions, faced off against the Kiwanis Club, which always seemed to be second fiddle.

That year many of the Little League World Champions were on Kiwanis. Both teams entered the game without a loss so the league championship was on the line. All the 1960 World Series coaches also refereed for the Pop Warner football league, and Dvorak was one of the refs for the Amvet-Kiwanis Club clash.

"As fate would have it, he would have to make probably the toughest call of his life," Amoroso said. After taking the lead and with time running out the Amvets kicked off to Joe Mormello who ran it back for what would have been the go-ahead touchdown.

"Dvorak's heart was surely with the underdog Kiwanis Cub team whose roster was filled with players he had bonded with throughout the quest. But Dvorak called it like he saw it. Mr. Dvorak was the sideline referee who said he, Mormello, had stepped out of bounds," Amoroso said. "It was a close call and as I watched from the sideline, as Mormello passed me and I stood on the line and watched him score. I never saw his foot hit the chalk. Mr. Dvorak stood by his call, amid the glow of the World Championship, having to rule against most of his championship team players. I saw first-hand after that day that it bothered him as to whether he made the right call in conversations he had with my Dad."

"For the dads of Levittown, Little League was the social gathering place in the brand-new community.

"The 1960 Levittown American Little League World Champions put Levittown on the map and in the history books," Amoroso said.

The Boosters

Among his memorabilia, Craig Eisenhart keeps a booklet with a bright red cover and the title: "1960 Levittown American Little League World Champs." It's the program from the awards banquet held at the end of the successful season at the Levittown Public Recreation Association (LPRA), and it's a testament to the excitement that rippled through Levittown that summer. The community itself was even younger than the All-Star players who had put Levittown on the map, and appreciative residents and businesses were eager boosters even if they had no personal or familial connection to the players.

The booklet has pictures of each member of the team, including the alternates, the coaches, and the scorekeeper. Their photographs are scattered across ten pages that are filled with advertisements from local businesses. In an era before big box chain stores, these mom-and-pop shopkeepers were bursting with civic pride and happy to be associated with a team of winners.

One ad reads: "Congratulations From 5 Points Diner, Bringing Joy to the Public As Did Our Little League Champions." Morrisville Gardens praised the team "on A Job Well Done." Compliments and kudos likewise came from Harry's Pest Control, Gene's Barbershop, Beck-Dougherty Mortuary, Tullytown Tavern, the Penn Valley Bowling League, Gregory's

Auto Body, Martin Expert Tree Service, Cattani's Poultry Market (offering "Fresh-Killed Poultry"), Blakely Laundry, Merc & Zanni Brush for Spray Painting, and dozens of others. The Meenan Oil Company (I played for Meenan Oil in the National League), which routinely sponsored a Little League team in the regular season, took out the lone full-page advertisement which eloquently stated the sentiment shared by much of the town:

"The good will and publicity which has been brought to our community by this team effort will never be able to be fully measured. The Meenan Oil Company will continue in the future, to sponsor Little League teams in the hope that they will help our young people to learn good sportsmanship and to become good citizens."

How About Some Cheerleaders?

The back inside cover of the pamphlet lent to me by Craig Eisenhart paid tribute to the "Levittown American Little League World Champion Cheer Leaders." Pictured are six twelve-year old girls. Each wears a wide smile, a corsage and a white bow just above the bangs in either a short curly bob or a straight pixie haircut. The caption beneath the photographs notes: "One of the big reasons of the Levittown American Little League's success and fame was the constant cheering of these six belles, who attended and kept up a steady cheer throughout each game and also presented each member with a kiss on their way out of the field after each victory."

A decade before girls were permitted to play Little League baseball, these six girls had decided that they would be part of the tournament playoffs. Marion Amoroso, daughter of the team's scorekeeper, remembered being at her home with her friend Louise Bellavita (Veith) and some other girls. "We were thinking the summer was going to be boring, thinking about what we were going to do for fun, and we all decided it would be fun to cheer. That's when our summer took on a life of its own by being cheerleaders."

In pre-game practices they developed cheers targeted at specific players for Levittown American, and during each game, they led the Levittown fans in chants and cheers.

"Even when I watch the Little League World Series today, it takes me back to that summer," said Cathy Bellavita (Richardson).

United by the shared goal of winning the Little League Championship, the girls developed a camaraderie among themselves just as the boys did. The community took notice of the contribution made by the young ladies. Cathy Bellavita remembered going door-to-door throughout Levittown neighborhoods to collect money to pay for their travel expenses to far-off baseball fields. She said she felt "like the whole town was behind us ... everybody was willing to give."

Little League teams and most baseball teams typically do not have cheerleaders, who are more likely associated with high school football teams. In fact, according to Marion Amoroso, "No other Little League World Series team before or since has ever had cheerleaders." The girls were breaking new ground just as the boys were, and for Amoroso that meant, "The excitement of being a part of something so unique and so special that has never been done again."

The chaperones for the cheerleaders were Mrs. Amoroso, Mrs. Diiorio, and Mrs. Trombino. They encouraged the girls to exhibit good sportsmanship. It was a challenging assignment for 12-year-olds when a world championship was on the line. But the girls showed grace and poise at the start of each game by approaching the opponent's bleachers to greet their rival's fans and perform a welcome cheer that Louise Bellavita could recite a half a century later:

> "Sit-in on a suitcase thumb-in a ride
> Just came over from the other side
> Hello (opposing team name) how do you do
> We're the American All Stars here to greet you
> And when the game is over
> And when we've reached the end
> We want you to know we will still be friends.
> (shook hands with people on the bleachers)
> Yeah (opposing team name)!"

The girls won their share of recognition. On August 28, 1960, the front page of the sports section in the *Williamsport Grit* featured a photograph of the Levittown cheerleaders in the front row of the grandstands, cheering their team on to victory.

At the post-season awards banquet, held in honor of Levittown American's success, the boys received trophies for their outstanding performance, along with team jackets and baseball bats signed by all the players. Then the cheerleaders were called up to the podium and one by one presented with an envelope which they were asked not to open until each girl had received hers. The anticipation mounted as the six girls collected their envelopes. Then they giddily unsealed them and pulled out their reward, gift certificates to charm school. Now, that might cause some eyeball rolling in the 21st century. But in 1960? "We all remember the feeling of sheer PRIDE!" exclaimed Marion Amoroso. "So happy to have been a part of this wonderful experience!"

The community, local businesses, cheerleaders, parents and coaches provided a solid network of boosters for the All-Stars. Another part of the network were grandparents. As a newly-minted town, carved from fields and pastures, Levittown was made up primarily of young men and women in their twenties and thirties.

Their own parents and extended families still lived for the most part in cities that were not well-connected by public transportation to the suburbs. It was an effort to get from the downtowns of Philadelphia and New Jersey cities to the relatively rural ball fields of Levittown and then to other cities and states. But plenty of grandparents made those trips to the delight of their grandsons. Even many of those who couldn't physically be at the games, provided pep talks and moral support that the grandsons carried onto the field.

Craig Eisenhart's grandparents, Henry and Mary Eisenhart, attended the post-season banquet, and Craig acknowledged their support by presenting them with two special balls that he had received that night. The elder Eisenharts recorded the moment in a note written on the inside cover of their grandson's booklet.

"Craig gave the small participant ball to his Mom, Mom Eisenhart, as long as she lives, then it returns to him. The regular ball with all 14 boys' names on to his Pop, Pop Eisenhart…I really and sincerely think sports is wonderful."

The ball now sits on Craig's bookshelf.

First Round in Levittown

On Saturday, July 23rd, the first round of the 1960 Little League All-Star World Series began. Lower Bucks County had 15 local teams competing in the first round of the All-Star tournament.

In Area A:

Levittown Western beat Levittown International	7-1
Pennridge beat Fairless Hills	12-1
Levittown American beat Levittown Continental	7-1
Pennsbury National beat Bristol Twsp National	5-3

In Area B:

Bristol Borough beat Pennsbury American	1-0
Morrisville beat Council Rock	2-1
Bristol Township American beat Trevose	6-2
Levittown National (bye)	

The Levittown and Bristol newspapers did not have sufficient manpower to individually cover and report on each of the games.

Levittown National was the winner of the previous District 21 Area Championship in 1959, and since there was an odd number of teams (15), Levittown National—the League that I played in, had a bye in this first round.

What we do know about that first American League All Star game was that on Saturday, July 23, Levittown American beat Levittown Continental, 7-1, and that the pitcher for American, Joe Mormello, tossed a one hitter. It was a warning signal to the other 5,000+ Little Leagues around the world of about what was going to happen over the next twelve games.

After the first round, the number of local teams was winnowed from 15 to eight, which was much more manageable for the sports staff of the Levittown and Bristol newspapers.

Second Round —
Levittown American's Bats Explode

On Monday, July 25 at the Morrisville field, Levittown American met Pennsbury National and pounded them 16-3. Levittown American started Julian Kalkstein on the mound and he pitched a one-hitter. The team hit five home runs. Mormello had two home runs, Joe Fioravanti, Tucker Schwartz and Rollie

Clark, hit one each. Here is the score by inning:

Levittown American
5 4 1 3 0 3 **16**
Pennsbury National
0 0 0 1 1 1 **3**

Craig Eisenhart remembered that Pennsbury National had a big kid on that team. "Doug Powell was his name," he said. "He had like 16 home runs or something like that and we thought these guys were going to kill us. But we beat them 16-3. That day I hit a ball off the outfield wall at Morrisville for a nice double." Powell was another great athlete and would play football as a running back at Pennsbury High.

Joe Fioravanti fondly remembered this game's string of home runs-capped by his homer. A little later in life, Joe would be elected by the Pennsbury High School students as President of the 1965 senior class and he would attend the University of Virginia on a football scholarship.

Joe liked being the clean-up hitter that batted 4th in the lineup and he was quite capable of popping one over the fence.

As far as bats exploding, Craig Eisenhart's whole life has been wrapped around baseball. He went to Juniata College for his undergraduate degree as a Bachelor of Science in Biology and to the University of Pittsburgh School of Dental Medicine. Currently, he is a retired dentist after 41 years of private practice. For the last 31 years, he's been a volunteer assistant baseball coach at Juniata College. He said, "I coached Little League and Teener League, for 14 years, and then with my experience in Little League, I kind of felt I owed it to the younger players."

The American-Pennsbury game left lasting impressions on both teams. David Morris, was the left fielder for the Pennsbury All-Star team. He batted in the number 3 slot. David "... remembered warming up and taking batting practice and I was ripping the ball pretty good in warm ups and I generally pulled the pitches to the left side of the field with the third baseman and shortstop and left fielder and over the left field fence" Morris said.

"I remember that Jules Kalkstein was pitching and he had that big kick and it intimidated me. I came to bat in the first inning with two outs. When they saw me coming to the plate the Levittown coaches screamed and realigned the shortstop and the second baseman to play way over to the left side of the field, with the second baseman directly behind second base and the outfielders realigned to the left also. I could hardly believe that the Levittown American coaches scouted me so closely during batting practice. The Levittown American coaches were very good. I did walk once and I got a hit later in that game and we scored a couple of times but we got pounded."

Third Round: Americans Win
Close One and Division A Title

For their third local game on July 28, Levittown American played Pennridge. In their first game of the Little League All-Star Tournament, Pennridge had played against Fairless Hills and won 12-1. In that game, Jack Detweiler was on the mound for Pennridge and he had a one-hit pitching effort with 2,000 fans in the stands. Detweiler struck out 12 batters and he hit two home runs. Surely, a 12-year-old pitcher was instructed to be very careful when he pitched to Detweiler. Game Two for Pennridge had their number two pitcher on the mound, giving Detweiler a rest. It also enabled him to prepare for pitching against Levittown American.

Game three against Pennridge was a very tough game for Levittown American. It turned out, as expected, to be a real pitcher's duel between American's Joe Mormello and Pennridge's Jack Detweiler. Levittown won the toss and elected to bat first. Levittown's Julian Kalkstein led off with a single. Mormello also singled and it scored Kalkstein, who had advanced on a wild pitch. Levittown started off with the lead. But that one run would not be enough.

Joe Mormello was on the mound. He gave up only one hit in the entire game and that was a single to Jack Detweiler in the second inning. After hitting the single, Detweiler advanced around the bases on two passed balls and a wild pitch. I have already mentioned the difficulty that any catcher would have stopping Mormello's fast ball if he got a little wild, and Detweiler took advantage of it. His run allowed Pennridge to tie the score, 1-1, in the bottom of the second inning.

To start the third inning, center fielder Jim Grauel came to the plate. Detweiler was one of those strong and dominant pitchers that an opposing team must have dreaded. But Grauel was up to the challenge. He rocketed one out of the ballpark to take a 2-1 lead. That home run ended the scoring. Mormello faced only 19 batters that game. Detweiler faced only 21 batters and gave up just three hits and two runs—very low numbers against a team that often scored in double digits in the tournament. This high-tension pitcher's duel was the type of game that Levittown American had to win if the players were going to be the *World Champions.*

Jim Grauel now lives in Nevada. He remembers that home run with pride and the importance that it had. Jim "also remembers growing up in Levittown along with my younger brother and two younger sisters. I am retired now but when I was in the work-force I was a computer technologist. I am a widower and I have a daughter and two grandchildren. My childhood in Levittown was wonderful. I played first base and center field and, along with baseball, I played football and basketball as the seasons rolled by."

Grauel did not stop with Little League. "I played Babe Ruth, Connie Mack, American Legion and High School baseball. After high school I joined the United States Marine Corp and I did serve in Vietnam. I do remember that my parents went to see John F. Kennedy at the Levittown Shopping Center and I remember when Walt Disney came to Levittown to dedicate a school that was named after him."

His memories of his coaches matched those of his teammates. "Great men and great with kids. Always very calm. Our coaches had fielding and batting practice every day that we did not have a game. The Little League World Series turned out to be my summer vacation.

"My parents were excited and happy for all of us and I believe it was the same for the other families and our community," he said.

Third Round: Levittown National Beats Bristol for Division B Title

While Levittown American was winning the District A division, Levittown National was winning the District B division with a 12-5 victory over Bristol Borough before 500 fans at the Fairless Hills field. I remember being at this game and cheering for my home team National.

Levittown National had 10 base hits including two home runs and they led 7-0 in the third inning. Bristol rallied for two runs in the fourth inning and three more in the fifth inning to boost the score to 7-5. Then Levittown National scored five more in the bottom of the fifth inning and effectively closed out the game.

Buddy Culbertson pitched the distance for National, although he got a bit wild in the fifth and sixth innings. Joe Schickling hit a home run with one on in the first inning to give National a 2-0 lead. An additional two runs were scored in that first inning on singles, an error, and a passed ball.

The three-run third inning was powered by doubles by Chuck Lumio, a single by Jack Jacobik, and a walk to Mike Hasness. The fifth inning saw National scoring five runs, with a home run by Bill O'Callahan and a couple of walks and wild pitches by Bristol.

As for coaching, National was managed by Mack Moore and Jim Gregory, while Bristol was managed by Dick Tosti and Tom Muffett.

Levittown National 12 vs. Bristol Borough 5

Bristol Borough	Posi-tion	At Bats	Runs	Hits	Levittown National	Posi-tion	At Bats	Runs	Hits
Runey	3b	4	1	1	O'Callahan	C	4	1	1
LaRosa	Ss	4	0	2	Culberton	P	4	1	1
Muffett	C	2	1	0	Schickling	Ss	3	2	2
Veretino	Ph	3	1	2	Axenroth	Lf	3	1	1
Russian	Rf-P	2	1	1	Hassness	1b	1	2	0
Zengel	Cf	1	1	0	Duncan	1b	1	1	1
Messila	2b	2	0	0	Flair	rf-cf	2	1	0
Coffman	1b	1	0	0	Jacobik	Cf	2	1	2
Dugan	1b	2	0	0	Platek	Rf	0	1	0
Tosti	Cf-P	3	0	0	Lumio	3b	3	1	2
					Gaineiri	2b	2	0	0
					Smith	2b	1	0	1
Totals		24	5	6			26	12	11

Bristol Borough   0 0 0 2 3 0 **5**
Levittown National 4 0 3 0 5 x **12**

Fourth Round—Showdown in Levittown

On Saturday, July 30, Levittown American squared off against Levittown National in front of an estimated 1,700 people, including me, at Levittown National's home field at Brook Park, about 200 yards from my home on Garden Lane. The winner of the game was going to be the District 21 Little League Champs.

Kalkstein was the first batter and opened the game with a single to left. The Americans followed Bob Dvorak's preference of always batting first and building an early lead. Chet Gardner struck out and Joe Mormello blasted one of Joe Schlickling's fast balls over the left field fence for a 2-0 lead. Schlickling settled down and retired 12 of the next 13 batters that he faced.

In the second inning the Nationals loaded the bases on walks but couldn't put runs on the board. Jack Jacobik beat out an infield hit in the fourth inning and Russ Flail was hit by a pitch. So National had men on first and second. Chuck Lumio batted next, and he hit the ball back to Kalkstein, who tried to get a force-out at third base, but he threw wildly. This allowed Jakobik to score and Flail and Lumio to advance to second and third.

Kalkstein was cool, and he struck out pinch hitter Jim Duncan. Bill O'Callahan whacked an infield ground ball and Flail tried to score but he was nailed at the plate. Kalkstein retired the side by striking out Buddy Culbertson.

In the fifth inning and with the score of 2-1, Schlickling lost control with two walks and a single and he was relieved by Russ Platek, who was tagged for two singles which resulted in three runs and a score of 5-1. For me, the game felt much closer than the score indicated.

For Levittown National the season ended abruptly.

Levittown American won District 21. It was a formidable achievement. The local competition proved worthy. Levittown American played well against some very good local all-star teams. That experience helped to prepare them to play for the Pennsylvania Sectional championship. But the toughness of those four local games gave Levittown American the confidence it needed to take on the rest of the world.

Levittown American 5 vs. Levittown National 1

Levittown American	Posi-tion	At Bats	Runs	Hits	Levittown National	Posi-tion	At Bats	Runs	Hits
Kalkstein	P	3	2	2	O' Callahan	C	4	0	0
Gardner	1b	3	0	1	Culberton	Ss	3	0	0
Mormello	Ss	3	1	3	Schickling	P-2b	3	0	1
Fioravanti	Rf	3	0	1	Axenroth	Lf	3	0	0
Bickel	3b	2	0	0	Hasness	1b	2	0	0
Saft	3b	1	0	0	Duncan	1b	2	0	0
Grauel	Cf	3	0	1	Flail	Rf	1	0	0
Griffith	Lf	1	0	0	Jacobik	Cf	2	1	1
Eisenhart	Lf	1	0	0	Platek	P	1	0	0
Fleming	C	1	1	0	Lumio	3b	1	0	0
Clark	2b	1	1	1	Gaineiri	2b	0	0	0
					Smith	2b	0	0	0
Totals		24	5	9			22	1	2

Levittown American 2 0 0 0 3 0 **5**
Levittown National 0 0 0 1 0 0 **1**

Memories of the Quest and Local Games

Steve Amoroso

Steve Amoroso was a 10-year-old during the Quest of the 1960 Levittown American Little League, but he participated by helping his father and the other coaches in fielding practice balls and pitching to Levittown American batters during batting practice, while learning and prepping for his chance to play on future all-star teams. He had three sisters, one older and two younger. His father was civic-minded and was Vice President of the Pennsbury School Board for many years. When I asked Steve about whether he served in Vietnam, he laughed and said he had the college exemption but when he was eligible to be drafted, his birthdate in that year's lottery was chosen as number 365 (talk about luck!), and the draft board only got up to calling number 112 that year for the young men to be drafted.

He remembers his childhood consisting of baseball, courtball, stickball, basketball at the pool, being there all the time and dealing with competition all day long. He remembers Levittown as an awesome place to grow up. Out from dawn to dusk. Other sports that he played were basketball and football, and he continued to play baseball through his second year of college.

Steve has baseball in his blood. Bucky Walters, who played baseball for the Phillies and the Cincinnati Reds, was Steve's mother's brother, otherwise known as "Uncle Bucky." He was a pitcher and was Most Valuable Player of the National League in 1939. Steve remembers "...being at his first professional game with

Uncle Bucky, who at the time—1956, was the pitching coach for the New York Giants, and Uncle Bucky took me to the Giants versus the Dodgers game. My biggest thrill was, before the game started, Uncle Bucky waved me down from the stands and introduced me to Willie Mays. I was all about baseball."

As far as making a living was concerned, Steve said that "For 15 years, I was a promoter, manager and agent in the music business. I promoted my first show in 1975, at the Trenton Speedway with Aerosmith, and special guest Kingfish. Bob Weir from the Grateful Dead was in this band. I managed Kingfish for four years in the 1970's. We were looking for talent in the music scene in Bucks County. Jody and I started a band in 1965, at 15, and played at the Cellar, underneath a deli in the Levittown Shopping Center. One of my great memories was meeting Jerry Garcia of the Grateful Dead and everything else paled. What he projected in his music was what he was like in real life.'

Steve said that he started his band in 1965 with Jody Giambelluca who was a street corner singer with the band Valentine in the first "Rocky" movie.

Craig Eisenhart

As far as bats exploding, Craig Eisenhart's whole life has been wrapped around baseball. He went to Juniata College, following in the footsteps of his father who was a student at Juniata from 1940-1944. Craig got his undergraduate degree as a Bachelor of Science in Biology and his dental degree at the University of Pittsburgh School of Dental Medicine. Currently, he is a retired dentist after 41 years of private practice. For the last 31 years, he's been a volunteer assistant baseball coach at Juniata College. He said, "I coached Little League and teener league, 13-14 years, and then with my experience in Little League, I kind of felt I owed it to the younger people."

I asked Craig to tell me about his father.

"My father has a most unusual story. During World War II, President Roosevelt deemed it desirable for professional baseball teams to continue playing as a public service to take peoples' minds off of the War."

"My father was a student at Juniata College. He had astigmatism and a strong eyeglass prescription, but boy could he pitch. In 1944, his Senior Year in Juniata, he memorized the eye chart so he could pass the Army physical."

"In Army boot camp, it didn't take long for the Army to realize that he couldn't see, and they put him in a hospital. He would leave the hospital to pitch for the camp's baseball team (near Richmond, Virginia). He pitched spectacularly for an Army guy and he received an honorable discharge."

"My Dad was quite the athlete. He was first team on the All-East NCAA Basketball team in 1944. He also pitched two one-hitters against the University of Pittsburgh's Baseball Team, same day, back to back I believe. Once out of the service, the Cincinnati Reds signed him to a 30-day contract and put him immediately into the Major Leagues ($500 bonus, guaranteed 30 days and one appearance)."

"Joe Nuxhall was another Reds signee. My father

made one Major League appearance on June 10, 1944. He relieved Joe Nuxhall in one of the most famous days in Major League history. Joe was 15 years old, and to this day he is the youngest player to play in Major League baseball history. The Reds were getting killed by the Cardinals in a game, and they put Joe in. He got two outs. Then, Stan Musial came to the plate. The story goes that Joe became buck-eggy and walked him and the next four batters. My father relieved Joe. He walked the first man he faced. Then he got Mort Cooper to pop out to second base to end the inning."

For the majority of us who have never heard the term *buck-eggy*, it refers to what happens when a deer hunter freezes up when he/she focuses the site of a rifle on a deer and the hunter gets stage fright and blows the shooting opportunity because he/she is too excited to shoot.

How did Major League Baseball react to war? In World War I, Major League Baseball was cancelled mid-season. In World War II, on January 15, 1942, Franklin D. Roosevelt wrote the "Green Light Letter" which supported the continuation of the upcoming Baseball season. Remember that the United States had recently entered World War II after Pearl Harbor was bombed and attacked by the Japanese on December 1941. Roosevelt wrote, "I honestly feel that it would be best for the country to keep baseball going. There will be fewer people unemployed and everybody will work longer hours and harder than ever before."

Those were welcome words.

"The Reds cut Joe and my father after the 30

days. Joe went back to high school. My father finished college, played a few years in the minor leagues and never made it back to the Majors."

"My father, J. Henry Eisenhart, taught Summer school in the Pennsbury system in 1960 and 1961. He pitched batting practice to us Little Leaguers when asked in both years."

Chapter 6

Levittown American Steps into Sectional Play

Little League founder, Carl Stotz, was either optimistic or hubristic in 1947, when he dubbed his first ever Little League championship the *World Series*. Of the 12 entrants, eight were from Williamsport and nearby, and three more were from the rest of Pennsylvania. It was a lone team from Hammonton, New Jersey, that enabled the event to catapult from a state tournament to a world series. Pennsylvania would remain a powerhouse in the league's formative years with World Series wins by Williamsport in 1947, Lock Haven in 1948, and Morrisville in 1955, when they were led to the Championship by Dick Hart.

The big break for Stotz came in 1949 when the *Saturday Evening Post* ran a feature on the Little League, and several newsreels picked up the story. Suddenly, Stotz was getting inundated with requests from around the country for information on how to start a Little League. The following year, a Houston, Texas team won the Little League World Series. Other championship teams in the 1950s hailed from Connecticut, New York, Alabama, New Mexico, and Michigan. In 1957 and 1958, a Mexican team claimed the top spot, finally, making the tournament a true *World Series.*

Also in 1957, Little League Baseball divided the US into four regions and the Pennsylvania State Champions were placed in a regional tournament against other state champs to get to the finals of the World Series. There was no standardized formula for how states or regions produced their winners, but Pennsylvania leagues were organized into 32 Districts that comprised eight Sections.

In the first round of sectional play after winning the District 21 tournament, Levittown American played Oreland before a crowd of 1,500 at West Norrington Field near Norristown, Pa. Levittown might have had the big bats and strong pitching arms, but in economic terms, it was the blue-collar community versus the blue-blooded one. Oreland is located in Montgomery County, due southwest of Philadelphia. It was originally settled as one of William Penn's manors, and one of its homes served for a month in 1777 as the headquarters of General George Washington. Today, Oreland remains an upscale community with an estimated median home price of $306,977, almost double the Pennsylvania median home price of $174,100.

The sectional play-off between Oreland and Levittown in 1960 represented the established patricians with deep roots and deeper pockets versus the brash newcomers from an upstart, instant community of cookie cutter homes. To players from Levittown American, the upper crust Oreland players were going to have the best bats and gloves and the nicest uniforms that money could buy. But money can't buy love, friendship, or happiness, nor in this case, a Little League Baseball victory.

For the fifth straight game, Bill Dvorak's team opted to bat first as they continued their sensational play. It was a good move. Levittown American scored four times in the top of the first and two in the second.

Joe Mormello, who was slated to pitch, was not feeling well. So Tucker Schwartz, pitcher number three, got his first start and first win in the Oreland game.

"I was the third pitcher," he said. "Jules and Joe were better than I, but the coaches gave me a chance to pitch. I did OK for four innings but they took me out and put Joe in to complete the game."

Schwartz did not begrudge his retirement after four innings. "Joe Mormello was amazing," he said, noting that the pitching ace struck out 16 in the final game. "And Julian Kalkstein had that great motion and he was smart."

Although he played only half the game, Schwartz recalled his tournament pitching start with affection. Like other Levittowners, both sports and academics would shape his young adulthood.

Tucker Schwartz was the starting pitcher and hung strong in the first two innings to get the win. In the third inning Schwartz gave up four runs. Joe Mormello, in a bit of bad luck for Oreland, relieved in the fourth inning after Oreland scored those four runs, and he finished the next two innings shutting Oreland out in the fifth and sixth innings.

Levittown American scored five runs in the last two innings to win the game 11-4. Levittown's big bats produced four home runs, two by Mormello and one each by Jules Kalkstein and Jim Grauel. The box score looked like this:

Levittown American 11 vs. Oreland 4

Levittown American	Position	At Bats	Runs	Hits	Oreland	Position	At Bats	Runs	Hits
Kalkstein	3b, ss	4	2	3	Girard	Lf	4	1	1
Gardner	1b	4	1	2	Schied	Cf	3	0	0
Mormello	Ss	3	2	3	Herr	1b	2	1	1
Fioravanti	Rf	4	3	1	Waterfield	Rf	3	0	1
Bickel	3b	2	0	0	Sinamon	C	3	0	0
Saft	3b	1	0	0	Barr	2b	2	0	0
Grauel	Cf	3	2	2	Edmister	Ss	3	0	1
Griffith	Lf	1	0	1	Savage	3b	2	1	0
Eisenhart	Lf	1	0	0	Van Hora	P	2	1	0
Fleming	C	1	1	0	Berry	P	1	0	1
Clark	2b	2	0	1					
Pennington	C	1	0	0					
Barto									
Schwartz	P								
Totals		24	11	13			25	4	5

Levittown American   4 2 0 0 1 4 **11**
Oreland   0 0 4 0 0 0 **4**

Although he played only half the game, Schwartz recalled his tournament pitching start with affection. Schwartz was smart as well. In fact, both sports and academics would shape his young adulthood. "I was a math major at Norwood University which was a military college. I played baseball all four years at Norwood," he said. At graduation he was given a commission in the Army and sent to West Germany. He would later become both a coach and a math teacher. In the summer of 1960, however, the numbers he was most concerned about were the ones on the scoreboard. And he took particular pride in the ones he was responsible for.

"I hit a home run in the Morrisville game," he recalled. "That was my standout play."

Although he's now retired, occasionally Schwartz will be called in as a substitute teacher. In the classroom, he sometimes imparts a bit of the Levittown Legacy to his students.

"In some classes I share my experience as a Little League world champion, and the kids enjoy it," he said.

Round 2 of Sectionals Played in Fairless Hills

For Levittown American, the second round of sectional play unfolded on a sunny late Saturday afternoon on August 6. Two thousand fans ringed the field in Fairless Hills to watch the home team Levittown American take on Cain Township.

American's expectations going into the game were tempered by Levittown National's previous years' experience. In 1959, Levittown National had likewise reached this point in the playoffs, only to be eliminated by Chester Suburban in a 5-2 loss. Chester Suburban went on to win the Pennsylvania State Championship that year. Now, a year later, Levittown American was facing a team that had already whipped Chester Suburban 9-5 in local play. In fact, Cain Township's victory over Chester Suburban was considered to be a big upset. Clearly, Cain Township would be no pushover.

Cain Township is in the heart of Chester County, (Southeast) Pennsylvania. Settlers from Calne Wiltshire in England arrived in 1714, and established what became Cain Township. The two towns, separated by an ocean, bill themselves as "Sister Cities." Once again, it was the Levittown upstarts challenging a team from an old community with a distinguished pedigree. The only tradition that Levittown American brought into the game was its penchant for being the visiting team and batting first.

Levittown American 8 vs. Cain Township 2

Levittown American	Position	At Bats	Runs	Hits	Cain Township	Position	At Bats	Runs	Hits
Kalkstein	P	2	2	2	Shiband	Lf	3	0	0
Gardner	1b	4	2	2	Ohar	P, cf	2	0	0
Mormello	Ss	3	0	0	Robinson	C	3	0	1
Fioravanti	Rf	3	0	1	Lynch	1b-p	3	0	0
Bickel	3b	3	1	2	Margolis	2b	2	1	0
Saft	3b	0	0	0	Smith	Ss	2	1	0
Grauel	cf,1b	3	1	0	DeLiota	3b	2	0	0
Griffith	lf-rf	3	1	2	Dunyer	Rf	1	0	0
Eisenhart	Lf	1	0	0	McCoberson	Rf	1	0	0
Flemming	C	2	0	0	Cochran	Cf	0	0	0
Clark	2b	1	1	0	Hickerman	1b	2	0	0
Pennington	C	1	0	0					
Barto									
Schwarz	Cf								
Totals		24	8	9			21	2	1

Levittown American   3 3 1 0 1 0 **8**
Cain Township   0 0 0 0 2 0 **2**

Kalkstein led off with a walk and scored with two more runs coming in the first inning. The game did not improve for Cain. American scored three more in the second inning and one each in the third and fifth innings. The final score was 8 to 2.

Kalkstein was the pitcher and he allowed only one hit and two runs. But the game was never in doubt. Although Kalkstein allowed two unearned runs in the fifth inning, he had a no-hitter going into the sixth inning until the opposing catcher, Clifton Robinson singled.

This victory secured the (District 21) Section 4 Title for Levittown American. The other winners in the second round of sectional play included: Section 1, Pittsburgh Hazlewood, Section 2, Punxsutawney Groundhog (District 10); and Section 3, Plains Township, (District 16). These four teams would now play for the State Championship.

The last two rounds of the State Championship in Pennsylvania would be played in Williamsport at Lamade Stadium, which was new in 1960. Each of these teams would get a taste of what it would be like to play in the final round of the Little League World Series. Only one of them, however, would survive this round of play. Levittown American was determined to be The One.

Levittown American In Williamsport

With the wins against Oreland and Cain Township, the Levittown Americans turned their attention to their three remaining rivals in Pennsylvania, knowing they would need to beat two of them to keep the Quest alive. The first opponent was the Section 3 champ, Plains Township, which is located in Luzerne County in northeast Pennsylvania's coal country.

One of the township's claims to fame was that it was the birthplace of Chicago White Sox pitcher Ed Walsh, whose illustrious career in the first and second decades of the 20th century propelled him into the

Major League's Baseball Hall of Fame. In fact, Walsh still holds the all-time record for career lowest ERA in Major League Baseball—1.82, accrued over a 14-year period from 1904 to 1917. Plains Township's Little Leaguers hoped to mentally and physically channel the skills of their hometown hero to a victory against Levittown American.

On Friday, August 12th, Levittown American was slated to meet Plains Township on Williamsport's beautiful new baseball field. It was the Little Leaguer's equivalent of playing in Yankee Stadium.

Exhilarated by the setting and elated to be on an overnight road trip, the Levittown American boys had trouble keeping their focus. The team had arrived in Williamsport the night before the playoff with Plains Township. The players and coaches were staying at Lycoming College in dorm rooms that had been vacated by students for the summer break.

It became apparent that a bunch of Levittown's young athletes did not know how to travel quietly, if they knew how to travel at all.

"The idea of all of us staying together, away from home, overnight, was so overwhelming that literally nobody slept," Joe Fioravanti told Bucks County Courier Times Sports Editor Dick Dougherty 25 years later. "Now, you can't field fifteen 12-year-olds with no sleep, not an hour, a half-hour, I mean none-at-all, without expecting to have difficulty. We ran all over that campus. We raised hell."

Craig Eisenhart remembers playing poker long into the evening.

The coaches, who also sat down for an interview with Dougherty 25 years later, had similar memories. Pitching Coach Roger Witt remembered that they were up at least past midnight and getting into mischief that was hard to control.

"They were throwing mattresses out the windows," he said.

It was a reputation that would follow them. Coach Bill Dvorak remembered that some of the state tournament officials caught players in a game of poker.

"We had to convince them these kids were all up-staters and it was a way of life with them." Dvorak told Dougherty. "They thought we were letting them gamble and were corrupting the morals of the kids." Then came regionals where officials in New York "…asked us to please make the kids behave. Please, please," Dvorak said.

It is easy to understand why that first sleepless night in Williamsport translated into an uncharacteristic struggle on the field the next day. "We played our poorest game," Fioravanti remembered. "We almost lost to a team that was not our equal because of the experience we had the night before, not sleeping."

Fioravanti also remembered that Plains Township put up a worthy fight that turned into an overtime thriller. Levittown American batted first, and took a 2-0 lead as Chet Gardner hit a two-run homer with Jules Kalkstein on base in the first inning. Gardner's home run was the first official home run hit in Lamade Field history. The ball was retrieved and placed on the shelf of the Little League Museum's historical files, where it is still on display today.

Levittown American had eight more hits for a total of 10 during the game. Plains had only three hits and scored a run in the fourth and a run in the fifth inning on pitcher/catcher mistakes. These errors allowed the base runners to advance to send the game into overtime. The sixth and seventh innings were uneventful. In the eighth inning, Rollie Clark, batting in the ninth slot, and Jules Kalkstein, batting first, put together back-to-back doubles scoring Clark. Mormello, given the lead, mowed down the three batters that he faced in the eighth inning to win the game. Mormello was the starting pitcher and he went all eight innings, striking out 20 batters. It's a staggering statistic given that over eight innings, the maximum amount of strike outs possible is 24. Mormello must have slept well the previous night. Plains Township had only four batters who either grounded or flied out. Mormello struck out 83% of the batters that had registered Levittown outs.

American was now one game away from being Pennsylvania State Champions.

Levittown American 3 vs. Plains Township 2

Levittown American	Posi-tion	At Bats	Runs	Hits	Plains Township	Posi-tion	At Bats	Runs	Hits
Kalkstein	3b	3	1	3	Grasanski	ss, p	2	0	0
Gardner	1b	4	1	1	Zhierski	1b	4	0	0
Mormello	p	3	0	0	Timko	cf,ss	4	1	2
Fioravanti	rf	3	0	2	Karia	P,cf	4	0	0
Bickel	3b	3	0	0	Rossi	3b	2	0	0
Saft	lf	1	0	0	Mastrini	2b	2	0	0
Grauel	cf	4	0	1	Dilandro	Ss	3	0	1
Griffith	lf	3	0	1	Wince	3b	2	1	0
Eisenhart	lf	0	0	0	Gemski	Rf	2	0	0
Fleming	c	4	0	1	Hreha	2b	2	0	0
Clark	2b	4	1	1	Wallace	C	3	0	0
Totals		32	3	10			30	2	3

Levittown American   2 0 0 0 0 0 0 1 **3**

Plains Township   0 0 0 1 1 0 0 0 **2**

The Groundhogs See a Shadow

While Section 3 and 4 Champs—Levittown American and Plains Township were battling in their 3-2 overtime final, the Section 1 Champions—Pittsburgh Hazleton was losing 2-1 to Section 2 Champions, the Punxsutawney Groundhogs. The Groundhogs beat Pittsburgh Hazelton largely because of the performance by the Groundhog's star pitcher, John Spinelli, who threw a two-hit complete game victory. Both Levittown and the Groundhogs won very

139

close games, each of which could have gone either way.

Punxsutawney is in Jefferson County, about 85 miles northeast of Pittsburgh. It's known as the weather capital of the world due to a groundhog named Punxsutawney Phil who, each February 2nd, becomes the country's most famous meteorologist. According to a Pennsylvania German superstition, if a groundhog sees its shadow due to sunny weather on that day, it will go back into hibernation and winter will last for six more weeks. Conversely, if cloud cover prevents the groundhog from seeing its shadow, Spring is expected to arrive early. Each Groundhog's Day, the town elders trot out a live groundhog supposedly awakened from its slumber in its burrow, Gobbler's Knob, and he is hoisted to a nearby stump.

The dark shadow that the Punxsutawney team saw on Saturday, August 13 in Williamsport was not cast by a groundhog. It was a warm, sunny afternoon when Levittown American met up with the Groundhogs in front of three thousand fans. As in the previous game, the difference would turn on the pitchers. Spinelli, the Hogs pitching ace, was not available to pitch against Levittown American. This is where Levittown reaped the rewards of having two strong pitchers. After a 20 strike-out performance, Mormello was giving his arm the mandatory rest and it was time for Jules Kalkstein to step in. The consistently solid Kalkstein overwhelmed the Groundhogs with his big-kick pitching style and accuracy.

Dvorak again opted to be the visiting team. In the first inning, Kalkstein tripled and scored to open the game. Kalkstein pitched a two-hitter complete game and American scored 2 runs each in the second, third, and fifth innings. Joe Fioravanti hit a two-run homer in the fifth, and Bickel added a couple of RBI singles. Below is the scorecard for the championship game in which Levittown tagged the Groundhogs with a 7-1 loss.

Levittown American 7 vs. Punxsutawney Groundhogs 1

Levittown American	Posi-tion	At Bats	Runs	Hits	Punxsu Hogs	Posi-tion	At Bats	Runs	Hits
Kalkstein	P	4	1	3	Neal	2b	2	0	0
Gardner	1b	3	0	0	D. Kaiser	Cf	3	0	0
Mormello	Ss	3	1	0	Strano	Rf	3	0	1
Fioravanti	Rf	3	2	2	S.Kaiser	Ss	3	0	0
Bickel	3b	2	0	2	Spinelli	C	2	1	0
Saft	3b	1	0	0	Milligan	1b	3	0	0
Grauel	Cf	2	1	1	Shafrom	3b	2	0	1
Griffith	Lf	2	0	0	Smith	Ph	1	0	0
Eisenhart	Cf	0	0	0	Davis	Lf	1	0	0
Fleming	C	2	1	1	White	P	1	0	0
Clark	2b	3	1	0	Pedell	P	1	0	0
Schwartz	lf	2	0	0	Cabell	Ph	0	0	0
Totals		27	7	9			24	1	2

Levittown American	1	2	2	0	2	0	**7**
Punxy Groundhogs	0	1	0	0	0	0	**1**

With its 8ᵗʰ straight win, Levittown American secured bragging rights and the Pennsylvania championship. Now it was time to take on the rest of America. But first, the team got a glimpse of what it was like to return to Levittown as conquering heroes.

Big Crowd Awaits Back Home

Levittown Cheerleader Louise Bellavita remembered that it was late at night and the players, coaches and cheerleaders were in a happy state of exhaustion on the way home. "We had to take the turnpike back home to the American League baseball field," she said. "It was late at night, perhaps 11:30 or midnight and it was a long turnpike ride home. Half of the bus was asleep and the other half was just quiet, all of a sudden, we were surrounded by police cars with their lights and sirens on."

The sleeping players were jolted awake. For a moment a current of alarm rippled through the bus. "We did not know what was happening at first," Bellavita said. "But then the adults on board told us we had a police escort from the PA State Police until we exited the turnpike and then the local police came and escorted us back to our home field. When we got to the field it appears that everyone, all of Levittown, was out to greet us."

Bellavita recalled, "The stands were filled with fans who had not been able to make the trip to Williamsport.

Others lined up around the fence of the baseball field. The field lights were on, and the P.A. System was on to welcome home the State Champs," Bellavita said. "Everyone was so tired but it was such a special moment for all us kids who were living our 15 minutes of fame, and it was just fun to be a part of it all."

One other detail has stuck with Bellavita, the bus driver's name. "The other thing I remember is the bus driver's name, it was Jim Winner," she said. "He was the bus driver who was pressed into service for all of the long-distance games.

"Every time we all got off the bus before an away baseball game, we would touch his name plate for good luck," Bellavita said. "Because he was a Winner and we believed that helped to make our team a winner and, in fact, it did."

Chapter 7

Traveling Onward to Eastern Regional Games

As the reigning Pennsylvania Champion, Levittown American represented Region 4 in the Eastern Regional Playoffs. In 1960, the Staten Island, New York Little League hosted the Eastern Regional Tournament at Hy Turkin Memorial Field on Staten Island. The field was named for an intrepid sportswriter for the *New York Daily News*. Turkin co-authored the first official *Encyclopedia of Baseball*, driven partly by his fascination with statistics. Had he lived to witness these 1960 Little League World Series games, they would provide the kind of stats that Turkin relished. And the best ones came from the Levittown Americans.

The tournament teams and coaches were housed at Wagner College for the long weekend that began on Thursday, August 18. The Levittown boys were surely wonderstruck by the setting. The campus was situated on the former 38-acre estate of shipping magnate, Sir Edward Cunard. For 30 years he was the agent of the steamer boats of New York, the Cunard Cruise Lines. Sir Edward, who was born in Canada, inherited his father's British title.

Wagner College overlooked New York harbor, Manhattan, and the Atlantic Ocean. The magnificence of these surroundings, however, did not prevent the Levittown boys from instigating some mischief that included tossing a mattress from a dorm window. In fact, the team would develop a bit of a reputation as little hooligans during their stay at Wagner College. Yet, it was their reputation for baseball talent that would leave a more lasting impression.

In their first game of the regional tournament, the Levittown American players faced the home town all-star team from Islip Little League. Islip is located on Long Island, just 20 miles from where William Levitt built his first planned community in 1947. But unlike either the Long Island or Pennsylvania Levittown, the town of Islip represented an older, more genteel establishment.

Islip was founded in 1683, and after an early start as a community of subsistence farmers, Islip steadily grew in prominence. By the mid-19th century, a fishing and tourist industry attracted New Yorkers and other city dwellers who vacationed at its seaside inns and dined on Blue Point oysters.

In the Gilded Age, wealthy New Yorkers including the Roosevelts and Vanderbilts, built summer mansions in Islip. Other brushes with celebrity in Islip came at the dawn of the motion picture era. The Vitagraph Company built a film studio in Islip. It was headed by Robert Ince, one of the most famous directors of the silent movie era, who worked with Errol Flynn, Douglas Fairbanks Jr., Ethel Barrymore, Boris Karloff, and other stars of the silver screen.

Following World War II, a housing shortage in New York City fueled a building spree on Long Island. Many of the men who spent their workdays in Manhattan settled their families across the Hudson Bay in towns like Islip. The ensuing population boom transformed the tourist and fishing hamlet. In 1960, when Levittown's small ballers met Islip's, it was a prestigious bedroom community of New York City. The white-collar Islip dads used their influence to convince New York City Mayor Robert Wagner to throw out the first pitch of the game. WPIX, the same television station that carried the New York Yankees, was on hand for a tape-delayed broadcast of the game. Some 3,500 fans filled the stands at Hy Turkin Field. Most of them were cheering for the hometown team.

What Levittown may have been lacking at the game in the numbers and financial status of its fans, it was made up for in collective lung capacity. The Levittown cheering section included Dads who knocked off work early from the factory, Moms who took a night off from cooking to make the 120-mile journey from Levittown, brothers and sisters of the players, and the Levittown baseball friends and fans, like my Dad and me, who were proud of this plucky and indomitable team. In front of the rowdy bleachers, the Levittown American cheerleaders led the chants of: "**LEV-IT-TOWN!**"

Levittown American No-Hits Islip, NY All-Stars

Levittown won the coin toss and again chose to be the visitors and bat first. Kalkstein led off the first inning with a single, stole second and scored on Joe Fioravanti's base-hit to take a 1-0 lead in the first.

In the third inning, Levittown American unleashed a home run attack. First, Julian Kalkstein homered over the center field wall. Next, Chet Gardner walked and was quickly brought home when Mormello also hit a home run in the center field area. Not to be outdone was Joe Fioravanti, who also popped one dead center out of the park. The three home runs in the third inning sealed the deal and took the steam out of Islip.

In the fifth inning, Fioravanti was driven home on a single by Brian Pennington. In the 6th inning Kalkstein doubled and Mormello doubled to score Kalkstein. Fioravanti got on base with an infield error and Jim Grauel smashed a three-run home run over the right field wall to finish the scoring.

Looking at the game stats for Kalkstein, Fioravanti and Mormello alone, Kalkstein had four hits and three runs, Fioravanti had two hits and three runs, and Mormello had two hits and two runs.

While Levittown's bats thundered, Islip's went silent.

Joe Mormello pitched a no-hit, no-run game and had 16 strike-outs as Levittown American beat the Islip, NY All Stars. Mormello walked three batters, hit two batters, and easily fielded two ground balls that were hit back to him. With 16 whiffs out of a potential 18 outs in a six-inning game, Levittown American's three outfielders and three of the infielders never had to touch the ball that afternoon—only the catcher, the first baseman and the pitcher handled the defense. Levittown American was not a very good guest of Islip.

Roger Witt, American's pitching coach, had been working with Mormello on a slow curve as an addition to his repertoire of pitches. Certainly, it must have worked pretty well in the no-hitter against Islip. Islip fans in the stands or watching the telecast on WPIX-TV, must have been shocked by the lopsided 10-0 outcome being seen by viewers throughout New York. This rout must have conveyed a strong message to American's next opponent, Newton, Massachusetts.

Levittown American 10 vs. Islip, New York 0

Levittown American	Position	At Bats	Runs	Hits	Islip, NY	Position	At Bats	Runs	Hits
Kalkstein	3b, 2	4	3	4	Veroziger	2b	1	0	0
Gardner	1b	3	1	1	Hoffman	1b,p	2	0	0
Mormello	P	4	2	2	Harsh	3b	2	0	0
Fioravanti	Rf	4	3	2	Menzi	rf,3b	3	0	0
Bickel	3b	3	0	0	Shabaum	P	2	0	0
Saft	lf	1	0	0	Unistock	Rf	1	0	0
Grauel	Cf	3	1	1	Holland	C	1	0	0
Griffith	Lf	2	0	1	Johnson	Lf	2	0	0
Eisenhart	Lf	0	0	0	Motto	Ss	2	0	0
Fleming	C	4	0	1	Mattera	Cf	2	0	0
Clark	2b	2	0	0					
Pennington	C	3	0	1					
Schwarz									
Totals		30	10	13			18	0	0

Levittown American 1 0 4 0 1 4 **10**
Islip, New York 0 0 0 0 0 0 **0**

Three Hits Against Newton, MA. to Regional Title

Newton, Massachusetts is a suburban city in Middlesex County, and it is located about 6 miles from the western part of Boston. It is bordered by West Roxbury, Brighton, Brookline and Wellesley.

It was settled in 1630 after relocating the Native American people of the Nonantum tribe who had lived there since time immemorial.

Like Islip, Newton was a community with deep roots in colonial America. Newton already was a century old at about the time that George Washington was born and its location so close to Boston put it near the epicenter of the American Revolution.

In 1934, Newton became a suburb of Boston when the Boston and Worcester train line reached Newton, making it easier for workers to commute into the city. Wealthy Boston businessmen could ride the railroad from their jobs in Boston to the less expensive, beautiful, and large-scale homes that were being built in Newton.

Newton shared more than just history with Boston. The route of the Boston Marathon, the nation's oldest road-running event, snakes through downtown Newton where runners must then climb four rises known as the Newton Hills. The fourth and best known is the fabled Heartbreak Hill, a steep half mile uphill that runners encounter at the 20-mile mark just when many are hitting their physical or mental "wall."

Traditionally, to cheer on the Boston marathon runners, Newton residents line the downtown streets

149

on Patriot's Day, which falls on the third Monday in April. One might think that the Newton West Little Leaguers had witnessed those struggling marathon athletes, and knew a thing or two about overcoming arduous challenges. But as it turned out, what they really needed to know about was heartbreak.

While Levittown was giving a licking to Islip, Newton West, one of two Little League All Star teams from Newton, Massachusetts, was squeezing out a nail-biter against an all-star team from Stratford, Connecticut. Pulling out a 7-6 win in extra innings, Newton West now entered the regional championship game against Levittown.

On August 20, Levittown American met Newton, Massachusetts in its 10th all-star game of the Quest. This second Regional game was also played on Staten Island with almost 4,000 fans attending. The pitcher for Levittown American was Julian Kalkstein. No surprise there. By now, all of American's opponents knew about Kalkstein's pitching delivery. Newton's coaches surely assigned batting practice pitchers and coaches to pitch with a similarly pronounced high leg kick so that the Newton players would learn how to see and bat against this unusual pitcher.

Levittown led off, as usual, and Kalkstein, as the leadoff hitter doubled into right field. Levittown's number two hitter did not get on base. Levittown's number three was Joe Mormello, who hit a 250-foot home run to jump out to a two-run first inning lead. It's usually a good sign when the pitchers are involved in a team's scoring offense. In the second inning,

American scored another run when Jim Grauel was hit by a pitch, followed by a passed ball, an error, and a balk that brought Grauel home for the score.

Newton countered. They scored when star catcher Joe Luchette homered in the second inning for their only run. It was Luchette's ninth home run in eleven All Star games and you can bet that Kalkstein was extremely careful when he pitched to Luchette again later in the game.

After crushing Islip with a no-hitter from Mormello and 13 hits and 10 runs from the team, something very strange happened. After the second inning, no one scored. Levittown's big bats went silent.

Newton's pitcher, Bob Gradon, was very effective, holding the Levittown team, which usually had its number of hits per game in double digits throughout the tournament, to record a total of only 3 hits, one each for the three best American League hitters for the whole game. Kalkstein doubled, Mormello homered, and Fioravanti singled.

Yet, Kalkstein's pitching was spectacular as he allowed only two hits—Luchette's solo home run and a single by Jeff MacLaughlin, Newton's third baseman.

There was no doubt that the team's reputation was spreading beyond the northeast and middle Atlantic States. The next day an article in the *Cincinnati Enquirer* reported that, "Levittown American won the Little League Eastern Regional title when one of the 'Bobbsey Twins,' Jules Kalkstein on the mound, beat Newton, Ma. 3-1. Kalkstein, known as 'Bibbsey' pitched his fourth straight two-hitter. The other Levittown right-hander, Joe Mormello—with a nickname of 'Bobbsey'--pitched a no-hitter against Islip in the semi-finals on Thursday."

Levittown American 3 vs. Newton Massachusetts 1

Levittown American	Position	At Bats	Runs	Hits	Newton Mass.	Position	At Bats	Runs	Hits
Kalkstein	3b,2b	3	1	1	Britt	2b	3	0	0
Gardner	1b	3	0	0	Chapton	Ss	3	0	0
Mormello	P	3	1	1	Perry	1b	3	0	0
Fiorvanti	Rf	3	0	1	Harwond	lf,cf	3	0	0
Bickel	3b	1	1	0	Luchette	C	2	1	1
Saft	Ph	1	0	0	Maclin	3b	2	0	1
Grauel	Cf	2	0	0	Clare	Rf	2	0	0
Griffith	Lf	2	0	0	Gradone	P	2	0	0
Eisenhart	Lf	0	0	0	Mullin	Cf	1	0	0
Fleming	C	0	0	0	DiRusso	Ph	1	0	0
Clark	2b	0	0	0	Keefe	Lf	0	0	0
Pennington	C	2	0	0					
Schwartz									
Totals		20	3	3			20	1	2

Levittown American	2 1 0 0 0 0 **3**
Newton, Mass	0 1 0 0 0 0 **1**

Having won its 10th All-Star game in a close call against Newton, Massachusetts, Levittown American now headed back to Williamsport—this time for the World Series Championship Games.

Chapter 8

Levittown American's Quest Leads to Gold

A stretch of the west branch of the Susquehanna River was once referred to as the "Long Reach" because there was almost no change in the elevation of the riverbed in the portion that runs through Williamsport. This feature made that section of the river an ideal location for a "log boom" a structure engineered to catch slow moving logs as they drifted downstream. The lush forests and the "Long Reach" were among the reasons that Williamsport became a major lumbering center in the 19th and early 20th centuries.

By 1960, the town had fallen on hard times. In the district known as Millionaire's Row for the lumber barons who had lived there, the once elegant mansions retained only a whiff of their former grandeur as they were mostly chopped up and sub-divided into low-cost rental properties. Their charm slowly decayed along with their chipped paint and rotting shutters.

But the romance of the Lumber Era was deeply

rooted in Williamsport lore. So, it was fitting that one of the institutions that eventually would help Williamsport rebound economically was the Little League organization and its World Series, whose first champion back in 1939 was Carl Stotz's team, Lundy Lumber.

For the eight teams who congregated in Williamsport on Sunday, August 21, the "Long Reach" had an entirely different meaning. Each team had won all 10 of their all-star games. They had defied the odds. Their Long Reach brought them from across the country and the world. The only "log boom" on their minds was the one they hoped to create with their big bats.

The teams representing the four domestic sections of the United States were: Levittown American, (Pennsylvania) East; New Boston Kiwanis, (Ohio) North; East Lakewood, (California) West; Fort Worth North East Optimist Club, (Texas) South.

Representing the international division of Little League were: Pearl Harbor (Hawaii) Pacific; Parkdale Little League, (Ottawa) Canada; Monterrey Industrial Little League (Mexico) Latin America; and Berlin Command Little League (Germany) Europe. Hawaii had just achieved statehood status the previous year in 1959, and it had not yet made the transition into the domestic division of Little League baseball.

The games began on Tuesday, August 23. The first match-up paired Levittown American against Pearl Harbor. As the Pennsylvania state champs, the Levittown boys were the hometown favorites. Their coaches, Bill Dvorak, Roger Witt, Chet Gardner and

Gene Amoroso, appreciated the boys' excitement. But they advised their team to play it *cool*. Throughout the tournament, the coaches would try to keep their players on an even keel, reining them in when they got too confident, and motivating them when they needed a boost.

Levittown American arrived in Williamsport with quite a reputation. The pitching duo of Julian Kalkstein/Joe Mormello had received a lot of news coverage. It was rumored that Mormello threw the fastest fast-ball that had ever been clocked in Little League competition. And Kalkstein's pitching delivery also was both reported in the press and probably was discussed and mimicked at rivals' practices. Opposing coaches were aware that in the 10 all-star games leading up to Williamsport, Levittown had scored 76 runs and had given up only 16 runs. No opponent was likely to defeat Levittown if Kalkstein and Mormello continued to throw no-hitters, one-hitters, or two-hitters.

Pearl Harbor Comes Under Attack

The Pearl Harbor Little League team had traveled more than 4700 miles from their home on Oahu Island in Hawaii. But their coaches were no strangers to Williamsport. Pearl Harbor had made an appearance in the 1958 World Series, where they were trounced in the first round 11-0 by Monterrey, Mexico, the team that went on to win the Championship and that was also making a return appearance in 1960. Over the years, Hawaii would field 12 teams in Williamsport including the 2018 Little League World Series champs from Honolulu.

Pearl Harbor's Little League tradition was rooted in the significant U.S. military presence in Hawaii. In the 1950s, while Hawaii was still a U.S. territory, Little League programs were started for the families of enlisted men and women. This included players that were the children of veterans from Hickam Air Force Base, Kaneohe Marine Corps Air Station, and Barbers Point Naval Air Station and for the families of locals who lived near or worked on the bases.

Until 1962, the Hawaiian leagues competed in a Pacific District tournament. Little League Baseball had become very popular in Japan in the post-World War II era, and the Japanese champion faced off against the top Hawaiian team for the right to represent the Pacific in Williamsport. In 1960, Pearl Harbor had emerged as the winner of the Pacific Tournament. Denied the championship once, they met the Levittown Americans on Tuesday, August 23, determined to take home the title that had eluded their predecessors in 1958. They surely had heard the hype about the scrappy players from Levittown. Still, they were not prepared for the blitzkrieg from the pitcher's mound.

Based on the previous performance of Joe Mormello and Pearl Harbor's Henry Salanoa, the game was expected to be a pitching duel. Salanoa was an imposing pitcher, a 5-feet, 10-inch and 157-pound right-hander, very big for a 12-year-old. According to the front page of the August 20, Sunday, *New York Times*, Mormello was said to be only five-foot-two inches and 108 pounds, a regular size for a 12-year-old. His fast-ball speed had been clocked in excess of 70 miles per hour—very fast for a Little League pitcher. Both pitchers had tremendous fast balls. But Mormello would prove to be—if not any faster, at least a lot more accurate.

Levittown won the toss, and as had become its tradition, elected to be the visiting team and bat first. No hits or runs were scored in that at bat. In the second inning, Brian Pennington and Rollie Clark both walked. Jules Kalkstein tripled off the wall in center field—200 feet out and both Pennington and Clark scored. In innings three and four nothing significant took place, leaving the score at 2-0.

In the fifth inning, Levittown scored again on a catcher's passed ball. Gardner walked and Mormello rocketed a ball to short center field for a single. Mormello advanced to second on the throw into the infield. And Gardner, who had stopped at third base, then scored.

In the sixth inning, Bickel walked and Griffith singled. Both runners advanced on a passed ball. Salanoa hit Pennington with a pitch in the shoulder and loaded the bases. Chris Mayne, a left-hander, was called in to relieve Salanoa and he struck out the next two batters. Then Chet Gardner hit a ground ball and the throw to second for the force out was botched by Pearl Harbor and two runs scored. Errors, walks, and hit batters can be killers for a Little League team, and

Levittown American had good catching, great fielding and accurate pitching. The team played a good, solid, conservative defensive game.

Mormello may have tired a bit in the sixth and allowed two runs to score before closing out the game. But those runs were soon forgotten by his teammates and coaches, because he tied an all-time Little League World Series record when he fanned 17 Pearl Harbor players.

Salanoa pitched strongly, he held Levittown American to only four hits and he struck out eleven American players. But he also pitched erratically, walking five and hitting three Levittown American batters.

The other Pearl Harbor putout (since Mormello had struck out 17 of the 18 possible outs) was on a shot by Lane Manuma, who in the fifth inning hit the ball deep to second base. Rollie Clark made a spectacular diving stop and rocketed the ball to Chet Gardner at first base to get Manuma for the out.

Overall, Levittown American had only four hits to Pearl Harbor's three. The 5-2 outcome was, in large part, due to walks, hit batters, errors, wild pitches and passed balls, the defensive part of the game. American was a bit lucky to have most of those catching and fielding mistakes go wrong for Pearl Harbor, and it did not affect the boys from Levittown.

Levittown American 5 vs. Pearl Harbor, Hawaii 2

Levittown American	Posi-tion	At Bats	Runs	Hits	Pearl Harbor	Posi-tion	At Bats	Runs	Hits
Kalkstein	3b	4	0	1	Caesar	Cf	2	1	1
Gardner	1b	3	1	1	Rosa	3b	3	1	1
Mormello	p	4	0	1	Cressford	Rf	3	0	0
Fioravanti	rf	1	0	0	Otterlei	C	3	0	1
Bickel	3b	1	1	0	Salanoa	P	3	0	0
Saft	ph	0	0	0	Manuma	2b	2	0	0
Grauel	cf	3	0	0	McCoy	Ss	0	0	0
Griffith	lf	3	1	1	Howard	Lf	2	0	0
Eisenhart	lf	0	0	0	Mayne	P	0	0	0
Fleming	c	0	0	0	Gable	Lf,ss	1	0	0
Clark	2b	2	1	0	Owens	1b	1	0	0
Pennington	C	1	1	0					
Schwartz									
Totals		22	5	4			20	2	3

Levittown American   0 2 0 0 1 2 **5**
Pearl Harbor   0 0 0 0 0 2 **2**

Levittown American Swamps Lakewood City, CA

In the semi-final game of the 1960 Little League World Series, the Levittown Americans faced a west coast team that in some ways was their mirror image. Like Levittown, Lakewood City, California, was a post-World War II suburb that emerged seemingly overnight from farm tracts on the outskirts of a bustling city.

Situated in Los Angeles County, the town was marketed to returning war veterans in search of modest homes in safe neighborhoods where they could raise their young families. Lakewood's 104 miles of streets, curbs, sidewalks, and street lamps proved perfect. Its recreational centers, ballparks, and playgrounds soon teemed with some 30,000 children, most too young, or involved in sports and other activities, to contribute to the narcotics and juvenile delinquency problems that plagued other cities at that time.

Like early Levittowners, Lakewood City's residents represented the demographic shift of blue-collar workers away from city-dwelling. The town was so youthful that a 1956 issue of *Kiwanis Magazine* claimed that Lakewood City had fewer mothers-in-law than any city in the country. Lakewood mothers, like their Levittown counterparts, no doubt told their children like my mother told me, that they could do anything, be anything that they wanted, because that was probably also the Lakewood Legacy.

In the mid-1950s, the new town had fought off an annexation attempt by neighboring Long Beach. In 1954, its young residents voted to incorporate, being the largest community in US history to become a self-governing city in one fell swoop. With no businesses or industry of its own, Lakewood contracted out for all its municipal services: police, firefighters, garbage collectors, dog catchers, etc. In the process, Lakewood City would be a model for homegrown cities around the country, just as Levittown was.

Lakewood City's growth spurt from a lima bean field to a sprawling suburb of 17,000 homes outstripped even Levittown's. In the initial three-year construction phase, a new house was completed every seven and one-half minutes. That added up to an average of about 50 new houses a day. The record, however, was a single day that saw the completion of 110 homes. Records mattered in Lakewood City. Competition mattered.

On August 25, Lakewood City met its match in Williamsport where it faced the youth of another instant city where competition mattered.

Julian Kalkstein was the star of this semi-final game which took place in front of almost 8,000 fans at Lamade Stadium. Lakewood could manage only two hits and one run off Kalkstein in the six innings that he pitched. He allowed both the one run and one hit in the first inning, but he settled down and allowed only one more hit and no runs over the next five innings.

Kalkstein was also swinging the bat ferociously, beginning with a lead-off single in the first inning. Joe Mormello, after he was hit by a pitch in the first inning, was driven home by Don Bickel's hard-hit single to left field. Lakewood's pitchers were having problems getting the ball over the plate and Levittown American scored three runs in the first inning.

Lakewood City could manage only two hits and one run off Kalkstein. In the first inning, Neil Younger of Lakewood got on base due to an error and advanced on a couple of wild pitches and a passed ball for Lakewood's only score of the day.

In the five-run fourth inning, Rollie Clark walked and Kalkstein hammered him home with a shot over the left field fence. Then, Mormello walked, Fioravanti walked, and Grauel got hit by a pitch—loading the bases. Bickel then walked, scoring Mormello.

The relief pitcher, Danny Beard, replaced the starting pitcher, Dick Nelson. Fioravanti scored on a passed ball and then Barto walked to again load the bases. Pennington hit a long fly ball to center field and Grauel tagged up and rocketed home to finish the scoring.

Kalkstein struck out nine, gave up two hits and he walked only two batters—an excellent performance. Although they **had only four hits**, two from Kalkstein and one each from Mormello and Bickel, the Levittown Americans won the game 9-1 thanks to seven big walks.

Levittown American 9, versus Lakewood City, CA 1

Levittown American	Position	At Bats	Runs	Hits	Lakewood City	Position	At Bats	Runs	Hits
Kalkstein	P	3	2	2	Younger	Cf	2	1	0
Gardner	1b	4	0	0	Knackert	rf	3	0	1
Mormello	Ss	3	3	1	Nelson	P, ss	2	0	0
Fioravanti	Rf	2	2	0	Cross	1b	3	0	1
Bickel	3b	3	0	1	Landler	lf	1	0	0
Barto	Lf	1	0	0	Lynch	Ss,3b	3	0	0
Grauel	Cf	3	1	0	Morzak	2b	3	0	0
Griffith	Lf	1	0	0	Beard	p	1	0	0
Eisenhart	Lf	1	0	0	Soberg	3b	1	0	0
Fleming	C	0	0	0	Murison	c	1	0	0
Clark	2b	1	1	0					
Pennington	C	1	0	0					
Barto									
Totals		23	9	4			20	1	2

Levittown American   3 1 0 5 0 0 **9**
Lakewood City, Calif.   1 0 0 0 0 0 **1**

Saturday, August 27th, was now slated to be Levittown American's date with destiny. The opponent took the form of the Fort Worth, Texas Little League All-Star team. In the other semi-final bracket, by the score of (5-1), Fort Worth had defeated Monterrey, Mexico which had won two of the previous Little League World Series Championships in 1957 and 1958. Mexico was seeking its third championship in four seasons, attempting a modified three-peat, a remarkable accomplishment.

Our Trip to Williamsport

My father had promised me that we would go to the Little League World Series Championship Game if Levittown American went that far. On that Saturday morning my mom packed up some food and drink for a day-long, round trip--driving from Levittown to Williamsport and back. She piled enough into the cooler to sustain me, my dad, and Uncle Leon. It was a rare boys' road trip, and I was happy to travel to the game.

Uncle Leon's wife, Aunt Lucille, stayed home with their daughter, Linda, and two younger sons, Bo and Clint, who were still toddlers. My six-year old sister, Bonnie Jean, stayed home with my mom. The women were content to watch the game on television.

The game was scheduled to air at approximately 4:45 PM on a video tape-delayed basis by WFIL, a television station in Philadelphia; directly following the Phillies-Chicago Cubs game. Curt Gowdy and Paul Christnas would be doing the play-by-play on ABC. It was the first Little League game to ever be televised nationally. I told my Mom to look for us in the stands. I was wrong. We couldn't get seats in the stands and we all sat in the grass past the outfield fence.

Our excursion to Williamsport would be a one-day, no-nonsense, round-trip. A motel room was not in our family budget. And it helped that there was no admission fee to get into the game. Driving costs were not an issue, I believe that the price of gas back in 1960 was about 25 cents per gallon.

We made the four-hour drive along mostly two-lane highways, that meandered through rural tracts of woodlands in north-central Pennsylvania. I nodded off occasionally, but each time I woke up, dad and Uncle Leon were still discussing the upcoming game, analyzing each player's strengths and weaknesses. I remember them talking about the grueling schedule the team had played and how the players and coaches were getting weary.

My dad fretted that fatigue could make the team sloppy and underperform its potential.

"Of course, all Little League baseball teams make mistakes." Uncle Leon had said. "And because of those mistakes they may lose games that they should have won." My father was talking like the true baseball coach that he was, understanding how pressure affects 10- to 12- year-old kids. He knew because he coached us and saw the way we performed under pressure.

Lying across the back seat of my dad's silver 1958 Chevy Impala, it sounded to me like my dad and Uncle Leon were preparing excuses in case Levittown American did not pull off a win. The best team doesn't always win, my dad concurred. The team that makes the fewer mistakes is generally the winner, that is often the determining factor in coming away with a Little League victory.

The Quest Ends—
Levittown American Brings Home the Gold

The front page of the August 28, 1960 edition of the *Williamsport Grit*, began: "The largest crowd ever to attend a Little League Baseball World Series game filled the stands of Howard J. Lamade Memorial field and spilled over on the surrounding banks to watch yesterday's championship game."

Countless hundreds of thousands and maybe even millions of viewers throughout the nation were watching the game on their television screens by way of a coast-to-coast television hook-up.

"With Joey pitching, we can't miss." Those were the first words out of the mouth of Julian Kalkstein after he was besieged by reporters and fans as the star of Levittown American's 9-1 victory over Lakewood City.

Pitching would again prove to be the key to success. An examination of the pitcher performances by both Levittown and Fort Worth make it clear that the principal reason these two teams had made it to the pinnacle of Little League play was their amazing pitchers.

Coming into the final, Levittown American's two starters, Mormello and Kalkstein, had given up a total of 14 runs in 12 tournament games. The two starting pitchers for Fort Worth, Texas—James Williams and Ronnie Reynolds, had given up only 11 runs in 12 games.

Mormello, besides being a great pitcher was also excellent with the bat, having hit 10 home runs in tournament play. Kalkstein, besides his outstanding pitching, had led off and scored the first run in eight of the games. At the plate, Kalkstein was 25 for 45, batting .555 with four home runs. Mormello, in addition to his 10 home runs had two doubles and two singles, had drawn a number of intentional walks, and he was frequently and probably intentionally hit by pitches— an opposing pitcher's painful way to move the batter back away from the plate. He had a batting average of .400. Those were spectacular batting numbers for a couple of pitchers.

In 1960, Fort Worth was hardly the "Wild West" of the era when cattlemen drove their livestock down the Chisolm Trail. In those days, a successful cattle drive was often celebrated in the saloons, brothels, and gambling dens of Fort Worth where many a cowboy was separated from his money.

Yet, the city's motto still identified Fort Worth as the place "Where the West begins." Town lore included stories of gunmen, sheriffs, shoot-outs, and colorful characters like Luke Short, a boxer, horse racer, and saloon keeper known for his excellent marksmanship. Once, when a waiter in a fine restaurant handed Short a glass of milk that had a small fly in it, Short was said to have calmly tossed the milk in the air, pulled out his pistol, and shot the fly in mid-air.

Fort Worth's 1960 Little League outfielders had seemingly dispatched flies with as much aplomb as their famous forbear, and the pitchers could claim Short's gift for finding his target. As the two teams took the field on a beautiful afternoon in Williamsport, it might have been a modern shoot-out of sorts. I remember seeing a few black Stetsons and I thought they looked pretty funny, protecting the heads of Fort Worth Dads from the brilliant sunshine on the afternoon of Saturday, August 27.

The old West with its storied past was taking on the new East, represented by an instant town with roots so shallow that the trees lining its streets were still saplings.

Media Coverage of the Championship Game

Sports writer Howard Tuckner led his front-page story on the August 28th Sunday *New York Times* like this: "Joseph Mormello Jr., a 12-year-old athlete from Levittown, PA. put the weight of his 108 pounds behind brilliant right-handed pitching today and produced

Joe Mormello pitching in the game and 25,00 people filling the stands in Williamsport

one of the finest performances in the history of the Little League world series today. A crowd of 20,000 sat spellbound at Lamade Memorial Field, as the 5-foot 2-inch pitcher unfurled the third no-hitter of the 14-year-old event. The victims desperately swinging from their heels throughout the game were the rangy lads from Fort Worth. Mormello, whose fast ball sped across the plate at more than seventy miles an hour struck out 16 of the Texans.

"The Don Drysdale of the sneaker set threw 83 pitches in the six-inning game. Sixty-two of them were strikes, all fast balls. Eleven of his strikeout victims went down with their bats knifing through the westerly breezes that played across the field." Through my 10-year-old eyes, the game unfolded more prosaically if no less emotionally.

Fort Worth won the coin toss and elected to bat first. Undoubtedly, the coaches of Fort Worth knew that Levittown American batted first in its twelve previous games and wanted to change things around for the final game. Could this be an omen?

In the top of the first inning, it went three up and three down for the Texans, nothing special there. In the bottom of the first inning, Chet Gardner singled and Joe Mormello hit a two-run homer that scored Gardner. I remember sitting on a blanket spread on the slightly rising grassy mound behind the left field fence at Lamade stadium. The home run that Mormello tagged landed close enough to us that I joined a mad scramble of kids to try to retrieve the ball.

Mormello rounding the bases with a home run as he stomps on the plate

But mostly I remember the thrill of watching those boys, just two years older than I was, and thinking that someday that might be me out on that field. They were my idols and role models. Not Pancho Herrera or Clay Dalrymple or Bobby Smith or the other major leaguers on the Philadelphia Phillies' roster. These Levittown boys were making history and I wanted to follow the path they had blazed to Williamsport.

Kalkstein continued the action in dramatic fashion with a home-run over the center field fence to open the third inning. Gardner then singled. Mormello was intentionally walked as Fort Worth did not want to see another home run off of his bat. Jim Grauel then doubled to left and knocked in two runs. That ended the scoring for Levittown American.

The *New York Times* article continued: "Today, Mormello needed little fielding support. Not a ball went out of the infield. The Fort Worth batter who should receive some kind of medal was Dave Hopper, who played third base and relieved Smiley Williams in the third inning. Hopper was the only Texan to hit the ball fair today. He grounded out to second in the second inning and to first in the fifth.

"Mormello, who has fanned 110 of 123 batters in the seven games that he has pitched in the tournament, lost his chance for a perfect game in the fourth when he walked Rickey Gaither. Mormello walked another batter with two out in the sixth inning. The first Fort Worth batter, Lewin Fullmer, worked Mormello for a 3-2 count before he went down swinging. The crowd roared. The next batter took three straight cuts and sat down. The crown was silent now. The Fort Worth manager had Dick Tergerson in as a pinch hitter. The count went to 3-2. The next pitch has high and outside.

"Steve Lacroix was Fort Worth's next pinch hitter. Mormello wound up. A ball. A swinging-strike. A called strike. Mormello tried a curve on the next pitch. It skipped past the catcher and Tergerson advanced to second. The crowd still was quiet. Mormello wound up again. Lacroix fouled it back. Now the tension became unbearable. One fan yelled, "Do it, Joey. Do it for me, kid."

"Mormello hurled a blinding fast ball right down the middle of the plate. Lacroix swung on. The ball was in the catcher's mitt before Lacroix had completed his swing.

"Levittown kids piled toward the mound from their fielding positions and the dugout. Mormello jumped into the arms of Brian Pennington, his 95-pound catcher. Flash bulbs popped. Mormello was a hero. But there also were other heroes for Levittown.

"There was Chet Gardner, the first baseman who got three hits. There was Jim Grauel, the sure-fielding center fielder, his double to left scored two runs in the third. And there was Rollie Clark, the 4-foot 6-inch second baseman whose constant stream of chatter encouraged Mormello throughout the day."

From Fort Worth's perspective, things were pretty boring in their dugout until Mormello walked Rickey Gaither. Gaither advanced to second on a passed ball and third on a wild pitch. With no outs and Gaither on third, Mormello did what he did best. He struck out Ronnie Caruthers, Billie Roberson, and Ronny Reynolds to end the threat.

Joe Mormello wound up throwing a no-hitter against Fort Worth. He also struck out 16 batters. At the end of six innings, Levittown American had won the 1960 Little League World Championship by the score of 5-0.

Tuckner reported that Mormello's fast ball was clocked at more than 70 miles per hour—extremely

Mormello carried out by his teammates after the no hitter in the final game

fast for a 12-year-old. As the Little League distance of 46 feet from the pitcher's mound to home plate, hitters had little chance to react to such speed. Mormello's 70-mile heater looked like a 90-mph fast ball from 46 feet.

The front sports page of the Sunday *Philadelphia Bulletin* had a picture of the entire Levittown American team holding a victory banner and a close-up photo of Joe Mormello delivering a pitch in the championship game.

The article in the *Bulletin* stated that, "His 16 strikeouts today and 17 against Pearl Harbor in the first round on Tuesday had exceeded a new World Series record—the old one being 31." Mormello pitched seven complete games in the tournament. "Of the 123 possible outs, he (Mormello) got 110 on strikes." He struck out 89% of the batters he faced. The final was his second no-hitter.

According to the *Bulletin*, "Joe's father, Joe Mormello, Senior has been grooming Joey in baseball since Joey was three. Joe Senior, a butcher by trade, was once a player in the farm system of the old St. Louis Browns." Obviously, Joe Mormello Senior did an excellent job in his development of the pitching skills of his son. Joe Mormello Junior struck out 16, walked two, and the Levittown defense was surprised when any Fort Worth batter put the ball into play.

With the last strikeout of the game, the Levittown American team, coming from the playing field and the dugout collapsed upon Joe Mormello as they celebrated their victory. The parents, who had the tears of joy streaming down their faces, jumped into congratulate their team member son. The fans flooded onto the field and celebrated this long-deserved victory. And the cheerleaders drank it all in as they led the cheers.

The quest was long and difficult, but worthwhile, as Levittown American was crowned the Little League World Champions. And they received the Championship Trophy, their Holy Grail.

Levittown American 5, versus Fort Worth, Texas 0

Levittown American	Position	At Bats	Runs	Hits	Fort Worth	Position	At Bats	Runs	Hits
Kalkstein	3b	3	1	1	Gaither	Cf	1	0	0
Gardner	1b	3	2	3	LaCroix	Ss	1	0	0
Mormello	p	2	2	1	Caruthers	Ss	2	0	0
Fioravanti	rf	3	0	1	Robinson	2-3b	2	0	0
Bickel	ss	3	0	0	Reynolds	C	2	0	0
Barto	lf	1	0	0	Hutton	Rf	2	0	0
Grauel	cf	3	0	1	Hooper	3b-p	2	0	0
Griffith	lf	2	0	0	Tipton	Lf	2	0	0
Eisenhart	lf	1	0	0	Fulmer	1b	2	0	0
Fleming	c	0	0	0	Williams	P	1	0	0
Clark	2b	2	0	0	Calmen	2b	1	0	0
Pennington	C	2	0	0					
Barto									
Totals		23	5	7			18	0	0

Fort Worth, Texas   0 0 0 0 0 0   **0**

Levittown American   2 0 3 0 0 x   **5**

Exhibit 2 shows the opponents and the game scores for the thirteen rounds of the 1960 Little League World All-Star Season. Levittown American won all 13 games.

Exhibit 2:
1960 Levittown American All-Star Game Records

Round	Opponent	Score
1	Levittown Continental	7-1
2	Pennsbury	16-3
3	Pennridge	3-1
4	Levittown National	5-1
5	Oreland	11-4
6	Cain Township	8-2
7	Plains Township	3-2
8	Punxsutawney Groundhogs	7-1
9	Islip, New York	10-0
10	Newton, Mass	3-1
11	Pearl Harbor, Hawaii	5-2
12	Lakewood City, California	9-1
13	Fort Worth, Texas	5-0

In aggregate, the total of the box scores for Levittown American's 13 games is 92 runs for and 19 runs against. Those are some pretty good numbers and a Little League World Championship to boot.

Chapter 9

Heroes of the Day—The Victory Parade

Lower Bucks County residents turned out in droves to celebrate the successful quest of the Levittown American Little League All-Star team. It was obvious that the players enjoyed all of the attention that they were receiving.

The front page of the August 29 edition of *The Levittown Times* proclaimed in huge type and caps: **"OVER 25,000 HAIL LITTLE LEAGUE WORLD CHAMPS IN 'WELCOME HOME,' Cheers Echo at Ball Field Ceremonies."**

The article began, "Cheering themselves hoarse for about two hours last night, more than 25,000 residents paid tribute to the world-champion Levittown American Little League Team."

According to the *Philadelphia Bulletin*, the celebration of Levittown American's Little League World Series Championship began at 7:00 PM at Magnolia Drive and ended at the Connie Mack Baseball field adjacent to the

Levittown Shopping Center at Levittown Parkway and Route 13. My dad and I were at the victory celebration, which began at 8:30 PM.

Jack Mack, President of the Levittown American League, introduced each player. The parade consisted of the players and coaches and several marching bands, baton twirlers, five local bands and a color guard to help with the welcomes.

"You mean they are going to give us a big celebration when we get home?" Joe Mormello asked. "That's great! That will be real fine with the fellows and me."

Neither Mormello nor any of his teammates were aware that the people of Levittown were watching the game as the victory unfolded. Mormello's Aunt, Mrs. Mackowsky said, "We watched the game over New York Channel 7. It was wonderful just to see those boys play the way they did. And that Joey, he smiled all the time. We saw on television Joey's father running out on the field after Joey threw the last pitch. It was really a party for everyone here and there."

Mormello's aunt said that she got "a hundred calls" from people in the neighborhood congratulating her on her nephew's achievement. "You know, it was funny watching Joey on television and I heard Joey's father shouting to the mound about every five seconds, we could hear him say, 'Come on Skip. Keep 'em comin, come on, Skip,'" she said.

The Bulletin noted that Mormello, Sr. had a great stake in his son's victory because he had been coaching his son in baseball since he was three.

"The older Mormello, a Merchantville, N.J. butcher, was once a player in the farm system of the old St. Louis Browns."

A fun fact here is that according to the *Philadelphia Bulletin*, Joey's Mother, Julia, known as Murph in the Mormello family circle, was once a circus acrobat who "liked the agonized contortions of the Texans trying to get at that fast ball."

Nearly 60 years later, I asked Julian Kalkstein what, if any, long term impact the World Championship had on him?

"It was a lot of success for such a young person," he replied. Quite frankly, I put it aside for many years. I had other things to do. School and then college were the key values instilled at home. One got on with one's life. Many, many years later my wife came across a picture of me pitching in the State championship game. She said let's put the picture out. That picture gives me a warm feeling. It represents a very exciting time in my life that I wish I had given more thought to over the years. I liked my coaches. I liked my teammates a great deal. It was a wonderful, wonderful time."

"A couple of years back," Kalkstein added, "I attended my 50th high school reunion. A slide presentation was made of the highlights of the class accomplishments of students, veterans, etc. The Little League Championship was included. Joe Fioravanti and I stood up and were acknowledged by our class. I was reminded of how good Levittown felt as a community about the team's accomplishment. The victory gave a very young town a very good feeling as demonstrated by the astounding size of the crowd at the celebratory parade. It has remained a fond memory and something as seen at my high school reunion, still held close by many."

Trip to New York City and Yankee Stadium

I had heard that the team made a trip to New York City to celebrate their world championship right after their victory parade. I asked Craig Eisenhart about it.

Eisenhart smiled. "This was only like a week after we won the World Championship. The Yankees invited us to go to Yankee Stadium. So we got on the bus, and my recollection was we had our uniforms on at that point. We drove to Yankee Stadium. The bus parked out in front, and we all walked in. We had lunch with the owner of the Yankees in the Stadium Club, and I have the ticket, and I have a letter from him and that picture that's over there. We all got interviewed by Casey Stengel. My recollection was that Casey had the bluest damn eyes. Nice guy. But you know like 70 years old. And we were like holy cow, this guy is old.

"We all lined up in the Yankee dugout and Mickey Mantle comes running into the field, throws his glove down, disappears and ran away. Didn't say a word to anybody. We were all upset." Yogi Berra was just as arrogant. But the players were happy to have their picture taken with Casey Stengel. Just before the Yankee's game against the Red Sox was due to begin does the same. I think Yogi at that point was catching. We got interviewed by Casey Stengel, and the Yankees took a picture of us with Casey."

"We got a message 5-10 minutes before game time that was delivered to the team. Ted Williams wanted us to go to the Boston Red Sox dugout. We all walked across home plate, all 14 of us. We get our picture taken with Ted Williams in the Boston Red Sox dugout. And Ted Williams signed my baseball in the dugout of the Yankee Stadium. And the press hated Ted Williams, he was prickly. But he was the nicest guy to us."

Another New York trip that Eisenhart remembered was a visit to the Topps Chewing Gum Company and the Hotel Manhattan. Every year Topps would have the top pictures on the All-Star Baseball team of Rookies, the all-stars, a little trophy on every card.

Each year, Topps had a banquet in the Hotel Manhattan. In 1960, Eisenhart said, "they had invited us, the Levittown American Baseball World Champions to present trophies to the 10 guys that were Professional Baseballs "Rookies of the Year." We all rode up on the chartered bus to Manhattan, had a banquet and got a signed ball. Mine burnt up when my house burned down."

Eisenhart said the company officials were nice to the team. Craig continued, "This was fantastic because those guys were nice to us. We were in the Hotel Manhattan, on the 27th floor within the Topp's Suite," he said. "Some of our guys thought they would start throwing ice cubes out the window. It wasn't too long till the police showed up in our room. Like, 'what the hell are you guys doing?' None of us got arrested. It wasn't the smartest thing we did. It was pretty darn stupid."

Craig notes that "Here is a story about my life much later. When I was on the Juniata College baseball team, we had a game in East Orange University against Upsilon College, which has now long been out of business. Literally, the game was on the day before the race riots started in Newark. We stayed in a downtown hotel, Hotel Newark, I think."

"My roommate was the only black member of our baseball team. And his name was Jim Day. We got to Newark, and we didn't play until the next day, we had a double header. Jim and I went out for a hot dog, and we just went, kind of walked aimlessly looking for a hot dog place. And Jim was bigger than I was, and I was 6'3" in those days. He kind of hit me in the elbow and said, 'I think we need to go back to the hotel.' He had a feeling that something bad was going to happen. And, honest to goodness, when we got done playing our games, 17 blocks of Newark were burning down as we were leaving town.

"It was that bad. And people now don't understand, this kind of relates to what's happening today. The country's got some problems right now, in my opinion, too much, I don't know, strife? But it was way worse in those days. JFK getting shot, Bobby Kennedy getting shot, Martin Luther King getting shot. The race riot in Levittown was really nothing compared to what happened five years later. And my baseball team came that close to being in the middle of that crap. Trenton had a big riot, Detroit. It was bad here for a couple of years."

"Do you remember the race riots in Levittown, Craig?"

"Yes. There was a black family that lived somewhere in Bristol Township. And it was very close to the James Buchanan elementary school that I was attending at that time. And I just remember it kind of started slowly and it just escalated. And it was a big thing in the newspaper. I don't remember exactly how it was resolved, though. I don't remember if the people stayed there or not. But I can remember seeing their picture in the paper.

"Well even if you tell me that, it was shocking to me when we went to Rome, Georgia, and we saw these signs about 'blacks at the back of the bus,' you know, different water fountains, blacks only, you know. And they might not have written *Negroes* at that point, I can't remember exactly that much. But it was really, segregation was a big thing. I personally was a Quaker."

"A Quaker! Really?"

"I just wasn't raised that way. For me it was particularly shocking."

"Tell me about being a Quaker, that's a lot less problematic than segregation."

"If I had to pick one tenet of religion it is 'if there is that of God in every man.' Historically, if you look at this as something, this is way off the charts, but there are those who denigrate Abraham Lincoln, because he was knowledgeable of genetics, as we are today. But anyway, Abe Lincoln, his grandfather was long dead when he was born, but he knew he was a Quaker. And I can't help but think, that maybe his Quaker belief was one of the reasons why Abraham Lincoln ended up signing the Emancipation Proclamation. That type of thing. But Quakers were very socially active, and that's just the way I was raised. I grew up in Bordentown. My father taught at Bordentown Military Institute (BMI). There were blacks that lived very close around the corner from us, and they were just part of my life from Day 1. It just didn't matter to me. And it didn't matter to my parents."

In Their Own Words

I have asked players and contributors to write "in their own words," about growing up in Levittown, about their playing Little League Baseball, and about their 1960 experiences.

Steve Amoroso

Young Steve Amoroso was a 10-year old during the Quest of the 1960 Levittown American Little League but he participated through his father in fielding practice balls and pitching to Levittown American batters during batting practice, while learning and prepping for his chance to try out and play on a later all-star team as an 11-year-old or 12-year-old. He had three sisters, one older and two that are younger.

Steve's father was civic minded and was Vice President of the Pennsbury School Board for many years. When I recently asked Steve about whether he served in Vietnam, he laughed and said he had the college exemption but when he was eligible to be drafted, his birthdate in that year's lottery was chosen as number 365 (talk about luck!), and the draft board only got up to calling the number 112 for young men to be drafted that year.

He remembers his childhood consisting of baseball, courtball, stickball, basketball at the pool—being there all the time and dealing with competition all day long. He remembers Levittown as an awesome place to grow up. Out from dawn to dusk. Other sports that he played were basketball and football and he continued to play baseball through his second year of college.

Steve has baseball in his blood. Bucky Walters, who played baseball for the Phillies and the Cincinnati Reds, was Steve's mother's brother, otherwise known as "Uncle Bucky." He was a pitcher and was Most Valuable Player of the National League in 1939. Steve remembers "...being at his first professional game with Uncle Bucky, who at the time, 1956, was the pitching coach for the New York Giants. Uncle Bucky took me to the Giants versus the Dodgers game. My biggest thrill was, before the game started, Uncle Bucky waved me down from the stands and introduced me to Willie Mays. I was all about baseball."

As far as an unusual way for making a living was concerned, Steve said that "For 15 years, I was a promoter, manager and agent in the music business.

I promoted my first show in 1975—at the Trenton Speedway with Aerosmith and special guest Kingfish. Bob Weir from the Grateful Dead was in this band. I managed Kingfish for four years in the 1970's. We were looking for talent in the music scene in Bucks County. Jody and I started a band in 1965, when I was 15, and played at the Cellar, underneath a deli in the Levittown Shopping Center. One of my great memories was meeting Jerry Garcia of the Grateful Dead and everything else paled. What he projected in his music was what he was like in real life."

Steve said that he started his band in 1965 with Jody Giambelluca who was a street corner singer with the band Valentine in the first "Rocky" movie.

Craig Eisenhart

"I come from a family of baseballers. Here is a story and it's a little bit crazy. It's kind of strange but is one about my father and it was 1944 and World War II was slowing down but it still was taking its toll on the United States and President Roosevelt declared he wanted baseball to continue to play to help occupy our minds and moods over duels on the playing field rather that the fields of war."

"The Cincinnati Reds scoured the country for five people who had never played professional baseball, not just minor league ball, but professional ball. My Father was one of those 5 guys that they signed along with a guy named Joe Nuxhall, and I think it was June 10, 1944 that the Reds were getting whomped pretty good and they ran Joe Nuxhall up there and he got to pitch.

According to Nuxhall's playing stats, he was 15 years, 10 months, and 11 days old, when he pitched in a regular professional baseball game, he became the youngest player ever to appear in a major league professional baseball game at any position.

Still to this day and probably forever, Nuxhall will have been the youngest pitcher ever to pitch in the major leagues. He got the first two outs and then walked the next 5 guys so the Reds coach pulled him and they put in my father, Jake Everhart, to relieve him."

"My father walked the first guy and got the next guy to pop out and the inning was over. In our family lore, we like to think of my dad's performance as a 'two-hitter.' All 5 of the guys had 30-day contracts and Nuxhall and my Dad were the only two guys to ever play. All five were quickly dropped by the Reds."

"My dad was later signed by the Trenton Spartans, which was in Class B ball as a farm team for the Philadelphia Athletics or Brooklyn Dodgers, I'm not sure which. He pitched in the minor leagues for three years or so. Then, he went on to being a school teacher in the Pennsbury School District."

As far as bats exploding, Craig Eisenhart's whole life has been wrapped around baseball. He went to Juniata College for his undergraduate degree as a Bachelor of Science in Biology and the University of Pittsburgh School of Dental Medicine. Currently, he is a retired dentist after 41 years of private practice. For the last 31 years, he's been a volunteer assistant baseball coach at Juniata College. He said, "I coached

Little League and teener league, 13-14 years, and then with my experience in Little League, I kind of felt I owed it to the younger people."

"Did you have any kids playing?"

"I had two sons who played. One daughter that didn't."

"So, you were coaching them?"

"I coached and played with them. Shoot Gary, I'm still playing. But I played with my sons up until two years ago. At that point, I was 67. They played in the Huntingdon City Baseball League."

"What do they do for a living?"

"My oldest son was a counselor at J.C. Blair Hospital in Huntingdon, Pa. My other son does wall boarding. He works a lot in State College, Lewistown, and around this part in Central PA. My daughter is a nurse in Altoona Regional Hospital, now known as UPMC Altoona."

Julian Kalkstein

"What memories do I have of the games leading up to Williamsport? It is hard to remember each of the games. I did get a kick out of the Islip, New York game that got us into the regional finals. Joe pitched a no-hitter, and four of us, Jim Grauel, Joe Fioravanti, Joey and I, we all had home runs! We were on top of the world.

"I was truly on top of the world because I was hitting and pitching. According to the "stats" of the games kept by my brother Josh, the guy who taught me how to play ball, I went 27 for 47 for an average of .575. I scored 22 runs and had 13 RBI's. It was a remarkable stretch. I was on a tear. When I went to the plate, I had tremendous confidence. It was a great feeling. I was always going to get a hit. Our team was a dynamo of run production, averaging 7 runs per game. Our opponents scored 19 runs or about 1.4 runs per game.

"I also pitched all of the championship games leading to the World Series: the Levittown championship game; the Pennsylvania sectional game; the Pennsylvania State championship game; and the Eastern United States championship game. I did not give up more than two hits in any of those four games. I went on to pitch the second World Series game.

I asked, "Do you remember any particularly close games where you pulled it out?" Julian answered that, "In the run-up to the State championship, we had a particularly exciting game against Plains Township. The game went into extra innings, tied 2-2. In the top of the eighth inning, with two outs, Rollie Clark hit a double. I was up next and I hit a double to right, sending Rollie home for what proved to be the winning run. Joe retired the side in the bottom of the eighth inning, recording a total of 20 strike outs (in the game).

Then, I asked a really difficult question for him. "What do you remember about your team's pitchers?" Julian laughed and answered that "Joey and I provided a powerful one-two punch for the team. Pitching for Little Leaguers can take on a greater role than it does for older players. He and I had tremendous success. I had a curve ball that my brother Josh had taught me. It was a difficult pitch to hit. Joey was a powerful fast ball pitcher. As stated previously, I had tremendous success in each of the game's leading up to the World Series and in the second game of the World Series. And Joey set a combined strike out record for the first game and the final game of the World Series.

I asked Julian if he could describe the excitement of his family or the community. "I think my folks tried to stay calm. They knew what was going on as we climbed the ladder of Local, State and Eastern United States championships. They tried to carry on and provide some sense of normalcy in the house. Only later did I learn from them how crazed and excited they and other families were as we proceeded to the World Series. My brother Josh kept meticulous stats of the games."

I asked, "What did your coaches tell you as you prepared for the championship?" Julian answered, "They didn't tell us anything in particular. We did not discuss the opposition. We continued our practice routines. I remember we practiced at an out of the way Little League field. Behind home plate was an announcer's booth. We somehow snuck in, turned on the speaker system and gave a play by play of the practice. We named the field "Bug Stadium." We had a lot of laughs. As these memories return, I realize that we were not a cocky team. We were not overly confident. We simply were a team that played hard, very hard every game. In between games, we had fun. One newspaper report has the team going swimming after we won the Series."

I asked, "Were you conscious of being a representative of Levittown?" Julian replied, "For sure, particularly when we reached the State Championship games. That feeling grew greater when we started to play teams from other states for the Eastern US Championship."

Further, I asked "At what point in the final game were you confident that you were going to win?"

"The newspapers record me saying right after the Lakewood game, that with Joey pitching we can't miss (winning the final game). Joey's record pitching stats in the two World Series games speaks for themselves. They are truly remarkable. Playing third base, I had an up-close view of his pitching. As I said before, he was extremely fast. He threw a very "heavy" fastball. He was very hard to hit. Batters were not fouling off his pitches, they were missing the ball altogether. He was poised. I felt confident that we would take the series with him pitching. Additionally, the team had been scoring a lot of runs in earlier games and we came to bat with a lot of confidence."

"What do you think was your biggest contribution to the wins?"

"I would rather answer this question as what was my greatest contribution to the team overall? I guess it was my hitting. Coach Dvorak came up with the very unorthodox notion of having our team bat first. Levittown batted first in 12 of the 13 games. We lost the coin toss in game thirteen and Texas chose to bat first. I led off each game. I believe that I got on base 9 times to lead off the 13 games. I was followed in the lineup by Chet Gardner, Joe Fioravanti, Joe Mormello and Jim Grauel, who all could hit. I scored often notching 22 runs in 13 games. I don't think we were ever behind."

Terry Nau

"I grew up in Fairless Hills, the next town over, and followed Levittown American's tournament success in 1960 with a mixture of envy and pride. Envy because many 12-year-old boys, myself included, still harbored hopes of becoming baseball stars, and Levittown American's players were already the talk of the town. Pride because Joe Mormello, Jules Kalkstein, Jimmy Grauel and most of their teammates were my classmates at William Penn Junior High. We were all very glad to see them when they came back to school in September.

"That championship marked those kids. I guess it put a fair amount of pressure on them as they tried out for sports teams and assimilated into our class of 725 students who would graduate from Pennsbury High in 1965. Some of them were really smart and goal-oriented, like our Class President, Joe Fioravanti. They all seemed to play at least one sport, sometimes two or more. As we grew up over the next four years and worked towards graduation, the Little League aura wore off. We all had bigger fish to fry in 1965. College, getting a job, hanging out with our friends. It was an exciting time to be alive.

"I was a mediocre baseball player whose career ended in American Legion ball at age 17, in the late spring of 1965. Because we all seemed to be interconnected back in those days, the last pitcher I faced in tryouts was Jules Kalkstein, still with the big windup, and very hard for me to hit. I remember hitting what I recall was a line drive to shortstop with my last swing. (It was probably a blooper.) After practice ended, the manager had some bad news, which released me to the sport of golf. I am forever thankful.

"At our 50th reunion, I walked over to Jules and kiddingly asked him what it felt like to peak at age 12. (Busting chops is something we grew up doing at Pennsbury.) Jules took my joke in good humor, thankfully. But I meant it with some seriousness. What Jules and his teammates accomplished in the summer of 1960 would live with them forever. Maybe achieving so much so soon propelled them to seek the same goals in the world. They showed us all that the sky is the limit.

"I was glad to hear Jules tell Gary Gray he has begun revisiting this wonderful memory of his youth, after a lifetime spent on more serious subjects. That reminded me of our Vietnam War veterans from the Class of 1965 who did the same thing, burying their memories and moving on with life after they came home. I recently interviewed Jimmy Grauel, who went to Nam as a Marine infantryman in 1966, just six years after winning the Little League World Series, and he was more focused on the clutch hits he got in the World Series than anything he did in the war. I guess we all remain kids at heart."

Tucker Schwartz

Tucker stated, "I lived on Evergreen Lane in Elderberry Pond and went to Pennsbury High. My father was a foreman at a chemical plant and my mother was a stay at home mom." While growing up he had an older sister and two younger brothers. He was a high school math teacher and coach.

Tucker remembers, "A very happy childhood, always playing outside. Riding our bikes everywhere. A very different world. Did a lot of fishing. Plenty of other kids around. I was nine when I started playing baseball. I loved basketball and also played soccer. I played from high school through college.

I was a math major and I had to stop playing soccer and basketball in my sophomore year in college. My university, Norwich University, was a military college. I played baseball all four years at Norwich. At graduation I was given a commission in the Army. I was stationed in West Germany.

Tucker added that, "My standout play was that I hit a home run in the Morrisville game. I was the third pitcher. Jules and Joe were better than I, but the coaches gave me a chance to pitch. I did OK for four innings but they took me out and put in Joe to complete the game.

"Joe Mormello was amazing. He struck out sixteen in the final game. Julian Kalkstein had that great motion and he was smart."

Tucker remembers, "Now that I am retired, I substitute teach, and in some classes I share my experience and the kids enjoy it."

Joseph Mark Fioravanti

Joe lived in Vermilion Hills and eventually went to Pennsbury High School. As he was reading my questionnaire, he stated: "My father was a stone mason and my mother worked at the Black Bass Inn in New Hope, Pennsylvania."

As an aside, "I, Gary Gray, the author of this book, have very fine memories of dining at the Black Bass Inn. I was living in Yardley and working as an investment banker in Philadelphia and New York City at the time. It was a very upscale restaurant, in a low-key manner, with a great menu and atmosphere."

Back to Joe. "I grew up with two sisters. I am married with three children and five grandchildren and I am a lawyer. I was elected by the Pennsbury High School students as President of the 1966 graduation class. I went to University of Virginia on a football scholarship and I attended the University of California, Hastings School of Law." Joe went on to be a prosecutor in the US Attorney's Office and later did criminal defense.

"I remember the coaches and the fathers that chipped in to help at our practices as very good role models. Yes, our practices were very hard work but we got lots of adult assistance. Baseball consumed that Summer." Fond memories were mixed with single-elimination baseball game tension.

"I was the clean-up hitter and batted fourth in the lineup and was quite capable of popping one over the fence. And I played right field on defense. I remember that first trip to Williamsport that the

Levittown American had taken for the Commonwealth Championship. The game was against Plains Township and went overtime into the seventh and eighth innings.

"It might be coincidence, but the night before the game the team stayed in the summer vacated dorm rooms of Lycoming College. Some of the knucklehead eleven and twelve years-old players stayed up all night keeping everyone else awake. The players got no to very little sleep which did not help our performance on the field against Plains Township. Luckily, in the top of the eighth inning Rollie Clark and Jules Kalkstein combined with back to back doubles to score. And given the lead, Joe Mormello overpowered the Plains batters in the bottom of the eighth inning to win the game."

One of Fioravanti's favorite memories was when Levittown American no-hit Islip in an Eastern Regional game when American unleashed a home run attack. Julian Kalkstein homered first. Then Joe Mormello rocketed one out of the ballpark. Then, in the same inning Fioravanti popped one over the center field wall and all three home runs in the same third inning ended up in approximately the same area.

Jim Grauel

I talked with Jim Grauel, who now lives in Nevada. He remembers very well that home run that he hit against Jack Detweiler of Pennridge and the importance that it had. In the third inning of Round 3 with the score of 1 to 1, center fielder, Jim Grauel came to the plate and he rocketed one of Detweiler's fast balls out of the ball park to take a 2-1 lead. The game then became a pitcher's duel and no one else scored.

Life does not come so easily. This high-tension pitcher's duel was the type of game that Levittown American had to win if the players were going to be the *World Champions*.

Jim "also remembers growing up in Levittown along with my younger brother and two younger sisters. I am retired now but when I was in the work-force I was a computer technologist. I am a widower and I have a daughter and two grandchildren. My childhood in Levittown was wonderful. I played first base and center field and, along with baseball, I played football and basketball as the seasons rolled on."

Grauel responded to my list of probing questions. "I played Babe Ruth, Connie Mack, American Legion and High School baseball. After high school I joined the United States Marine Corp and I did serve in Vietnam. I do remember that my parents went to see John F. Kennedy at the Levittown Shopping Center and I remember when Walt Disney came to Levittown to dedicate a school that was named after him."

He remembers that his coaches were: "Great men and great with kids. Always very calm." They had "… fielding and batting practice every day that we did not have a game." The Little League World Series "…this was my vacation."

Jim remembers "…all of the family and fan support that the team received." And as far as standout plays were concerned, he "… hit the winning home run in the District final. We won 2-1." He also notes:

"My parents were very excited and happy for all of us and I believe it was the same for the other families and our community."

And I piped in: "You did pretty well in the final game." Jim said, "I hit a bases-loaded two-run double and we won the game 5-0." It doesn't get any better than that!

How About Some Cheerleaders?

Louise Bellavita

Louise remembers growing up in the Elderberry section of Levittown with a large hard-working, middle class family with five siblings, including her *younger* (by several minutes) twin sister, Cathy. Her father was a book keeper/salesman for a brick company in Tullytown.

She is married with two children and three grandchildren. Professionally, she was a credit supervisor, HR director, and an insurance claims adjuster. "I remember Levittown as pure fun. Lots of friends (baby boomers), it was safe and secure, fruit trees in our yard, the Magnolia Pool across the street, Saint Michael's Fair, walking to the Levittown shopping center- Pomeroy's, SunRay Drug Store with lime Rickies. Little League field was across the street also located near the Magnolia Pool.

"I never played baseball, but my Dad, Louis Bellavita, was a coach for one of the Little League teams and my twin sister and I as 12-year-old girls would take great joy in seeing all the boys come pick up their uniforms and seeing the roster. We attended every game, no matter who was playing, as part of our summer nights. We would all hang out at the ball field watching the games and waiting for the games to end and see all the boys.

"After being such loyal fans and friends of some of the baseball players, we decided it would be fun to cheer them on! We bought our own uniforms and started to make up cheers to say at the games. We decided our trademark would be to wear bows in our hair and after every game we presented each player with a kiss on their way off the field. There were six 12-year-old girls who thought it would be fun to follow the team. That's how we became the *cheerleaders* for the All Stars."

"We cheerleaders had Moms who were our chaperones. Mrs. Amoroso, Mrs. DiOreo and Mrs. Brady made sure all the girls had a ride to the games and later we were permitted to ride on the team bus. It was one of my greatest summers ever! Try to imagine a group of young girls who decided to follow their hometown All-Star team through the long journey to the Little League World Series and making it all the way to Williamsport PA!"

"Being a small part of the winning of the 1960 Little League World Series has given me a lot in my life. It's bragging rights to my grandson whose All-Star team *only* made it to States. It's allowed me to share the "something you did not know about me" story in various business meetings. Last but not least it made a hell of a writing when returning to the eighth grade in the 'What did you do this summer' essay. All kidding aside, it was a beautiful experience that I am so happy I had in my life."

Thank you, Louise Bellavita!

Marion Amoroso

Marion Amoroso remembers "The excitement of being a part of something so unique and so special that has never been done again. No other World Series team before or since have ever had cheerleaders." Marion also remembered us sitting at her house thinking the summer was going to be boring, thinking about what we were going to do for fun, and we all decided it would be fun to cheer. That's when our summer took on a life of its own by just being cheerleaders. Marion remembers feeling like we were bringing the community together for one purpose. All of us remember the feeling of sheer PRIDE! So happy to have been a part of this wonderful experience!"

"The parade around Levittown was awesome! Here were six convertible cars that drove us down Levittown parkway, one girl with two boys sitting on the top of the back seat. That was the first time I learned the *queen's wave,* above the pearls below the crown. We ended up at the Levittown Shopping Center and there we and the team were presented with a trophy. All of us girls were given a certificate to attend charm school to teach us the finer things that young ladies should know. It was just an added bonus to a wonderful summer. I personally never felt like a hero because I was not a player but I felt very lucky and honored to be part of a journey that no other girls had been part of."

Cathy Bellavita

Cathy Bellavita (Richardson) remembers the experience for "the camaraderie, and an overall great summer. Even when I watch the Little League World Series today it takes me back to that summer."

Cathy remembers, "a banquet that was given to the All-Stars and the Cheerleaders at the LPRA (Levittown Public Recreation Association). Special trophies were given to the players and that is when each girl was presented with an envelope with a certificate to Charm School. Each girl was asked to wait to open the envelope until we all got them and open it at the same time."

She remembers "Feeling like the whole town was behind us, even when we went door to door everybody was willing to give." Cathy also remembers that the cheerleaders went out between innings and did cheers.

Chapter 10

The Aftermath: Levittown American 1961—
The Legacy Lives On!

Selection of the 1961 All-Star Team

The 1961 American League regular season must have felt like a warm-up for the American League players who planned to win a slot on the 1961 All-Star team. According to Dennis Pesci, the memory of the 1960 triumph galvanized players throughout the 1961 regular season. There were 17 slots, and more than ever, every American League player wanted one. As a result, Pesci said, they worked harder and trained more diligently.

The competition for the All-Star team in 1961 was intense. The 1961 players were trying to elevate their performance levels during the regular baseball season in hopes of making the all-star team. Many players felt, or wished, that they would be back in Williamsport in August and again playing for the Little League World Championship.

Some of the players, like last year's four 11-year-old All-Star teammates, experienced the all-star games playing at the highest levels and know first-hand about Levittown A's history in All-Star games. This year's competition for slots would be strong. In 1960, the players walked into a situation where they had terrific talent and no one else knew it.

Not this time. In 1961, Levittown American was a name that evoked dread among rivals. The 1961 players had a fearsome reputation to live up to.

The tryouts for the 1961 All-Star team were contentious. Since the players of Levittown A have tasted the fruit before, the 1961 players wanted to relive the success that they had in 1960. The three top picks were players who had made the 1960 All-Star team as 11-year-olds: Craig Eisenhart, Chet Gardner, and Gary Saft. They were the seasoned veterans, and they were prepared to lead their team to a repeat championship. The coaches knew these three played well under pressure, and they knew that the pressure would be more intense in 1961 because the expectations were so high.

The next most important grouping was the pitchers. No one believed that any player in 1961 could come close to pitching and performing like the 1960 stalwarts. Joe Mormello, with his stunning fast ball, had struck out about 90% of the all-star batters that he faced in the World Series games. Julian Kalkstein was unbeatable with his repertoire of curves and off-speed pitches, along with a vicious fast ball. Yet, the 1961 Levittown American team had three very good pitchers in Dennis Pesci, Sam Gumbert, and Chris Yates, all throwing to a solid catcher, Elliott Greenberg.

The 1961 team had some superior hitting in Tony Gervasio, Dan Brewster, Craig Eisenhart, Chet Gardner, Gary Saft, Dennis Pesci, Mike Goad, and Chris Yates. But fielding was where the 1961 All-Stars stood out. It was an excellent defensive team. It's hard to say whether the defense was better than the 1960 team, because the 1960 Levittown defenders did not have many opportunities to make tough defensive plays with Joe Mormello on the mound striking out 90% of the batters that he faced and Julian Kalkstein with his delivery intimidating opponents. If a player strikes out, he can't hurt you.

Dan Brewster, George Strickler, and Mike Pierce contributed defensive aspects as needed. The team was chosen! They now would practice four hours per day to get ready to play against the best teams in the world.

Dennis Pesci remembers that 1961 Quest of the Levittown American Little League All-Stars. He was one of the three Levittown pitchers that propelled the 1961 team up to the Little League World Series in Williamsport. Later in life he would serve in Vietnam from January 1969 to January 1970. He was stationed at Cam Rhan Bay in Vietnam and he was the crew chief on a C7A Caribou.

The coaching line-up was likewise a mix of the 1960 alums and some new faces. As one measure of the attention focused on the 1961 All-Stars, the media was following them even in their pre-season. *The Bucks County Courier Times*, in an August 17th story, profiled the coaches starting with Chet Gardner, Sr. who became the team manager in 1961. He was a 38-year-old employee of a trucking company, and his son, Chet Junior, was the team's first baseman.

"Gardner believes that when a team reaches championship playoffs like the 1960 team, the players have achieved the apex of their ability within their age limits. To keep them performing at peak, he will on occasion *chew* a boy out. "I insist they hustle, but you can't push a boy too hard or you'll hurt his morale. I try to use psychology. Some boys need pushing a bit, other's do not."

"Gardner believes the biggest problem in keeping his team on the victory trail is keeping their spirits and confidence at a high pitch." He doesn't worry about his kids getting cocky. "We like it," he says, "a confident boy can fire up his teammates. Against Punxatauney, Gary Saft, our third basemen, got the team fired up when we were down 2-0 and coming to bat for the last time. The boys won 4-2."

Gardner understands, "Being behind in a game can break the boy's spirit. Older boys don't crack under this particular pressure, but it's tough on the 11 and 12 years-old Little Leaguers."

Coach Joe Fioravanti, Senior was also profiled. He was 40 years old and lived in Vermillion Hills, and his son, Joe Junior, was on the 1960 World Champion team. "Joe Fioravanti, Senior is a mason by trade. He played baseball in high school in the service and in sandlots," the article noted.

Charles Cantwell, Senior, was a 36-year-old coach

whose son Charles Junior was a Little Leaguer. He was employed by the US Steel Fairless Hills Works and had spent four years working with Levittown American Little League. He was the manager of the Watson and Schwartz Insurance Company Little League team.

According to *the Courier Times* article, the coaches did not appear to like the terms *Manager* or *Coach*. When they refer to themselves, they use the term *Adult in Charge*.

Dennis Pesci described the coaches as, "Really good dedicated people. They gave so much of their time. They really worked with us and taught us baseball."

Much of the above description of the coaches and the quotations are taken from an August 17, 1961 *Bucks County Courier Times* article titled *Meet the Levittown 'Skippers'*.

The 1961 Games

The Local Games

Round 1: Saturday, July 22, 1961- Levittown American earned a bye due to winning the District 21 championship in 1960 and due to an uneven number of teams in the District.

Round 2: Tuesday, July 25, 1961- (8-2) Levittown American took on the winner of the Council Rock-Pennsbury game, which was a powerful Council Rock team, at 6:00 PM at Magnolia Park field. Winning pitcher Chris Yates gave up only 3 hits and Yates, Dennis Pesci, and Gary Saft each had two hits for Levittown American, which won 8-2. The defending world champs scored in each of the first four innings as they coasted to an easy victory.

Round 3: Thursday, July 27, 1961- (5-0) Levittown American beat Bristol Borough by the score of 5-0 before 400 fans at Morrisville Little League Field. Through four innings, the game was scoreless. The Levittown pitcher was Dennis Pesci who did not walk a batter and was opposed by Tom Carpenter, the pitcher of Bristol Borough, who struck out 12 Levittown batters. Craig Eisenhart led off the scoring barrage when he hit a 200-foot home run over the center field wall with one on in the fifth. And Levittown American scored three more in the sixth to shutout Bristol Borough, in an otherwise close game.

Round 4: Saturday, July 29, 1961- (11-1) Levittown American met Bristol Township American at Fairless Hills and hammered them 11-1, and the 1960 veterans launched an impressive five home runs. Chet Gardner, the elder, was the voice of the "adults in charge" who handled the defending Little League World Champs and he said, "I knew we had the home run power, but I just didn't know when they would open up." On a smallish size, Sam Gumbert @ 4'11" and 93 pounds struck out nine and walked only one as Gumbert shot Bristol Township down with his off speed and curve balls. Gumbert allowed only four hits. Vince Scarcella started for Bristol Township. Levittown countered with a two-run homer by Gary Saft in the first inning, a two-run blast by Chet Gardner in the third inning, and a two-run homer by Craig Eisenhart in the fourth inning.

Power in the form of Craig Eisenhart-one home run and one triple; Chet Gardner-two home runs; and Gary Saft-two home runs; the big three 12 years-old holdovers from the 1960 World Champion team, reared their heads and pounded Bristol Township American (11-1) for the District 21 championship.

The Commonwealth Games

Round 5: Tuesday, August 1, 1961- (3-0) Levittown American beat Broomall 3-0 before 1,200 fans at Media, Pennsylvania. Dennis Pesci, at 5 foot 4 inches and 106 pounds fired a three hitter. From the newspaper sources that reported, there was a tremendous defensive effort in this game. The Levittown American fielders threw out two runners as they tried to stretch for extra bases and the Levittown A's played error free baseball.

Round 6: Wednesday, August 2, 1961- (4-0) Levittown American beat Plymouth Township 4-0 in front of 1,200 fans at Upper Moreland Field in Willow Grove, Pennsylvania. Husky 110- pound 5-foot 4-inch Mike Farrell pitched for Plymouth Township. Levittown American could only manufacture three hits. Levittown pitcher Sam Gumbert yielded 8 hits to Plymouth Township, but he got some more excellent defensive support to preserve his 4-0 shutout win. Levittown had three hits and their opponents had eight hits and Levittown American won (4-0) in a shutout? How crazy is that! With the win over Plymouth Township, Levittown American recorded their 18th win in a row in Little League All-Star play. Those 18 games included 13 games from the 1960 team, and it beat the 17-game winning streak that Monterrey, Mexico set in 1957 and 1958.

Round 7: Friday, August 4, 1961- (9-3) Mahanoy City in Freemansburg, PA had just beaten West Chester East Side Optimists 4-0. On August 6, 1961, Levittown American won its 19th straight tourney victory by beating District 24's champion Mahanoy City 9-3 before 2,000 fans at Freemansburg. Levittown had 13 hits and two home runs in beating Mahanoy City. Levittown got its first five runs in the first inning. Chris Yates, with a 5-foot 9-inch and 125-pound build, pitched a five-hitter. Both Dennis Pesci and Mike Goad hit home runs.

Round 8: Friday, August 11, 1961- (4-1) Levittown American 4-hit Bentleyville and won the game 4-1 before 3,000 fans at Olmsted Air Force Base in Middletown, PA. Behind the pitching of 4 foot, 11-inch, 93-pound Sam Gumbert, who was insulted by a Bentleyville player who asked, "Hey kid, what position do you play?" Gumbert responded that, "You'll find out tomorrow." True to his word, Gumbert pitched strongly, struck out four and did not walk a batter. Bentleyville's pitcher Brown struck out eight American Leaguer's and walked only one. Mike Goad hit a home run in the fourth inning and Dennis Pesci scored American's fourth and last run with a big 230-foot home run in the sixth inning.

Round 9: Saturday, August 12, 1961- (4-2) Over a two-year period and twenty-one All Star games, the Levittown American Little League All-Star **never ever had to come from behind in any inning to win a baseball game**. That changed on Saturday, August 12 at Olmsted Air Force Base in Middletown, Pennsylvania. The Levittown American team overcame a 0-2 deficit in the sixth inning against the Punxsutawney Groundhogs and again won the State Championship 4-2 in front of 6,000 rabid fans.

The Groundhogs with their big 5'8", 153-pound pitcher Bill Sherry, were in control and had shut Levittown out for the first five innings. The Groundhogs were leading 2-0 going into the sixth inning. The Groundhogs had an extremely powerful pitching combination, similar to Levittown Americans 1960 combo of Joe Mormello and Jules Kalkstein. Along with Sherry, they had Rodney White who pitched the Groundhogs to a 1-0 victory in their previous game against Hazelton, PA.

Dennis Pesci took over the pitching for Levittown American in the second inning with Levittown down 0-2. He struck out 12 batters over the rest of the game. "I was a little scared at first, but now I'm really happy,"

Pesci said after the game. Levittowner, Tony Gervasio had two hits in the game including a game winning two-run single in the sixth inning. In the newspaper account, Gervasio said, "I was scared when I went up to bat and was more scared on each pitch. With two strikes I was even more scared but I just did what the manager said and I got the game winning hit."

Levittown American, the defending State Champion, finally had to come from behind and beat a team—the Punxsutawney Groundhogs. The Americans were up to the challenge when they scored four runs in the sixth inning to beat the Groundhogs 4-2.

According to the August 13 edition of the *Bristol Courier* and the *Levittown Times*, in the sixth inning, Chet Gardner walked and went to second on a wild pitch and scored on Gary Saft's double. Saft then scored on Denny Pesci's single to center. Mike Goad walked and Elliott Greenberg hit a slow roller and was out at first which moved Goad to second and Pesci to third. Pesci scored on a single by Tony Gervasio. Goad came home on a passed ball. The Gophers gave up those four runs in the sixth inning and Levittown American finally was able to prove itself by coming from behind to win the game 4-2 against the Gophers.

The Regional Games

Round 10: Friday, August 18th- (14-0) Levittown American 14, Brockton North, Mass 0. The Eastern

Regionals in 1961 was in Haddon Heights, New Jersey, only about 14 miles from Levittown.

In the first round of Regional playoffs, the Levittown American batters showed up and pummeled Brockton, Mass. 14-0. Samuel Gumbert was the pitcher for Levittown American and he allowed only five hits and recorded 13 strike outs while walking only one batter. Craig Eisenhart drove in five runs with a 2-run homer and a bases loaded triple.

In the first inning, Tony Gervasio singled and Eisenhart homered with a shot over the left field fence. In the second inning Levittown American scored three runs. Mike Goad got on base on an error by the shortstop—and he advanced on a passed ball. Elliott Greenberg singled to center. Gervasio drew a walk. Eisenhart then tripled to left field and the three runners on base scored.

With two outs in the fourth inning, Gumbert beat out an infield hit and Gervasio doubled to right and scored Gumbert. Brockton intentionally walked Eisenhart and pitched to Gardner who hit a home run scoring three runs. In the fifth inning, George Strickler singled and then Elliott Greenberg popped a 180-foot bullet over the fence in center field adding two more scores.

With Brockton changing pitchers to Welch, he had some problems with the feisty American League batters. Chet Gardner walked. Dennis Pesci hit a home run over the center field fence. Mike Goad doubled to left and advanced to third on a passed ball and scored the 14th run on another passed ball. Levittown American could do no wrong! "Craig Eisenhart had five RBI's while Chet Gardner had three RBI's and Dennis Pesci and Elliott Greenberg each had two RBI's."

Greenberg also hit a home run. With a great resumè from the team's performance at the first round of Eastern Regionals, Levittown American seemed to be the team to beat in Regionals.

Brockton had five hits and no runs.

Round 11: Sunday, August 20th- (8-0) Levittown American 8, Darien, Connecticut 0, the second and final round of the 1961 Eastern Regionals was played. According to the Levittown Times, "The defending Little League world champion used the home run on Saturday to defeat Darien, Conn. (8-0), and won the Eastern Regional play-off at Haddon Heights, N.J. before 4,000 fans. Levittown will now play in the first round of the world championship playoff at Williamsport, PA which starts Tuesday, August 22. Levittown American has earned its repeat trip to Williamsport.

"Chet Gardner, son of the Levittown manager, hit two home runs to drive in five runs, while winning pitcher, Dennis Pesci hit a two-run homer and Mike Goad hit a solo clout to account for all the Pennsylvanian's runs."

"While the power was turned on, Pesci held Darien to four hits, fanned 10 and walked two. A five-run first inning put the game on ice as Gardner got his first round-tripper, following an error, and then a single by Craig Eisenhart. Pesci slammed his homer after a double by Gary Saft."

"Goad hit his home run in the fifth and Gardner closed out the scoring with his second clout after a walk to Tony Gervasio in the sixth."

Dennis Pesci noted that his father worked for Rohm and Haas and his mother worked at Penns Valley Elementary School. Dennis is still very actively involved in baseball in Lower Bucks County. His son and daughter both went to Pennsbury High and his son is now the head baseball coach at Pennsbury High School. His son's team won their first 6A State Championship in Pennsylvania in 2017.

1961 Williamsport Little League World Series

Round 12: Tuesday, August 23rd- Levittown American 0, El Cajon, California 1, (0-1). The Heartbreaker! On this day in Williamsport in the first of the 1961 Little League World Series final three games, El Cajon, California beat Levittown American 1-0. It was the first-time in 24 tournament games that the Levittown American All-Star Team wound up a loser.

El Cajon had a great resume, having played nine games against California teams including two other El Cajon all-star teams (American and National). They also played a team from Rapid City, South Dakota and Concord, Nevada. They shut out 8 all-star teams, won 3 one-run games, and 1 two-run game and had an aggregate score of 59-5. From El Cajon's baseball history, it was probable that Levittown American may have some difficulty scoring against El Cajon. That is exactly what happened.

Dennis Pesci started the game at pitcher for Levittown American, and in the second inning he was hit by a pitch thrown by Mike Salvator, the El Cajon pitcher. Joe Fioravante, Junior was up in Williamsport cheering on his fellow ex-teammates and he is quoted as saying: "That pitcher (Mike Salvator) is the best pitcher in the tourney." He was right! After being hit, Dennis Pesci would not be able to continue to pitch and he was replaced on the mound by Sam Gumbert, Levittown American's curve ball artist who took over in the second inning.

Gumbert performed spectacularly and struck out 10 California players and had allowed only one hit during regulation play. The game went into overtime and in the seventh inning with one out Dennis Pesci stroked a single to right field. Next, Elliott Greenberg was safe on an infield error and Pesci advanced to third base. Unfortunately, a bunt by Mike Goad was laid down a little too hard and Salvator threw Pesci out at the plate.

Salvator's style of play was reminiscent of Joe Mormello in that he relied heavily on his fast ball to overwhelm opposing batters. Against Levittown American, he struck out 11 players and he allowed only three hits—Chris Yates had two hits and Dennis Pesci got the third hit. But Levittown A couldn't string together enough hits, walks, hit by pitches, passed balls and balks to break into a positive run scored.

Levittown American was shutout by Mike Salvator!

The Levittown Times notes that "Todd Lieber smashed a home run over the left field fence in the bottom of the seventh inning to give El Cajon, California, a 1-0 victory over the Levittown Americans in the opening game of the 1961 Little League World Series here today. Levittown which had won 10 straight games this year in tourney play and 23 over a two-year span, was eliminated by Lieber's extra-inning circuit clout."

Craig Eisenhart, a player on both the 1960 and 1961 teams, who is quoted in a *Bucks County Courier Times* article 25 years later on Thursday, August 21, 1986, as saying, "I still remember it even today. A kid named Todd Lieber hit the home run. He hit that ball between the left fielder and me in center field, and I can still see that sucker just clearing the fence."

The two-inch headlines from page 1 of the Tuesday evening, August 22, 1961, edition of the Levittown Times, price seven cents, read:

LEVITTOWN LOSES IN OVERTIME: Calif. Wins 1-0 on HR in Seventh

Dick Dougherty of the *Bucks County Courier Times* wrote: "Todd Lieber smashed a home run over the left field fence in the bottom of the seventh inning to give El Cajon, California, a big victory over the Levittown Americans in the opening of the 1961 World Series here today.

"Levittown, which had won 10 straight games this year in tourney play and 23 over a two-year span was eliminated by Lieber's extra-inning circuit clout." However, the 23-game winning streak is still Little League's All-Star Baseball's longest win streak.

Both Salvator and Gumbert were pitching spectacularly. Base hits and runs were tough to get with these two on the mound. The game was tied 0-0 at the end of regulation, that is the sixth inning in Little League play. A lot of players were striking out.

In the seventh inning, Todd Lieber, El Cajon's 5-foot, 7-inch 135-pound first baseman got a hold of one of Gumbert's rare hanging curve balls and powered a line drive 200-foot home run over the left field fence.

Levittown Americans finally had lost a game!

Levittown American lost to El Cajon, 0-1, in the seventh inning of the Round 12 of the 1961 Little League World Championship. Only four other teams, including El Cajon, Texas, would go onto the semi-finals of the All-Star Tournament this 1961 year and arguably will have done better that year than Levittown American. In fact, El Cajon won the 1961 World Series Championship, beating Hawaii 3-2 in the semi-final round, and they won the final game against El Campo Little League from El Campo, Texas by the score of 4-2. In Williamsport, El Cajon had played and won three very tough, low-scoring games!

And with the Levittown Americans, the players and the coaches and the parents and the other significant contributors, the sun again came up on Sunday and life still continued onward and upward.

Exhibit 3: Levittown American 1961 Game Scores

Round	Opponent	Score
1	Bye	
2	Council Rock	8-2
3	Bristol Borough	5-0
4	Bristol Township American	11-1
5	Broomall, PA	3-0
6	Plymouth Township, PA	4-0
7	Mahanoy City, PA	9-3
8	Bentleyville, PA	4-1
9	Punxsutawney, PA	4-2
10	Brockton North, Mass	14-0
11	Darien, Conn	8-0
12	El Cajon, California	0-1

The total box scores for Levittown American's 12 games amount to 70 runs for and 10 against with 5 shutouts. Some pretty good numbers! Unfortunately, El Cajon stopped short Levittown American's goal of winning back to back Little League World Series Championships.

Epilogue

The Levittown Legacy in 1961

Competition matters! That has been shown by both the 1960 and 1961 Levittown American All-Star teams. The 1960 team brimmed with talent, especially at the pitcher position, and arguably was the best team on the field during their thirteen game 1960 World Championship run. I believe that with Mormello and Kalkstein pitching, the 1960 players were almost unbeatable. They expected to win, and they did. They never had to come from behind at the end of every inning that they played.

The Adults in Charge of the 1961 team were pleasantly surprised with the play of the 1961 pitchers – Sam Gumbert, Chris Yates, and Dennis Pesci were all so good. The 1961 Levittown American's pitchers shut out five all-star teams and no team scored more than three runs against them. The 1960 pitchers recorded only two shutouts.

The Levittown Legacy may have been more important to the 1961 team than the 1960 team. Even the 1961 Coaching Staff has admitted that they thought that the 1961 team was not as talent-laden as the 1960 team. But I do not believe that any other Little League team has ever had that much talent.

But remember that baseball is a funny game. The best teams in the Major Leagues are very happy with a 65% won/loss record. In baseball there are so many moving parts and they don't always move together! In Little League baseball, the 1960 and 1961 All-Star teams won 100% of their games or the 1961 team went home.

The 1961 team lost to a very good opponent with the pitcher, Mike Salvador, and home run hitter, Todd Lieber, leading the way for the El Cajon, California Little League team. El Cajon ultimately won the 1961 World Championship.

Could the Levittown Legacy have intervened in stopping Todd Lieber's homer or in helping Levittown American to score a run earlier in that extra inning game?

I don't think of the Legacy as a spirit or as a miracle producer, which would enable an athlete to perform beyond his/her capabilities to miraculously hit the home run, or if he/she outruns a faster opponent to score the touchdown that wins the football game.

For that matter, the Legacy affects the female and male players of softball or of soccer or of basketball. I think that it is a belief that is built up by and for a person in a very competitive athletic environment. And that Legacy is due to his/her competitive nature and to the extent of their level of training and hard work that the players, or the attorneys (Julian Kalkstein and Joe Fioravante), or the Dentist (Craig Eisenhart) or the Chiropractor (Joe Mormello) or to the soldiers (Mormello and Barto and Grauel and Pesci), or the teachers/professors/ business men that have invested in themselves to compete favorably in their academic, military, or corporate practices.

Before I started writing this book, I had never thought about linking success in the athletic world directly with success in the business world, or the academic world, or in the legal world.

The town of Levittown and the environment in which I grew up, I now believe helped to lay the groundwork for me and for many of my friend's successes. Being small, short and slow are not the best of attributes for a football player, but by being very smart, I made up for my deficiencies and became an Academic All-American linebacker at Penn State.

I am sad to say that I have lost touch with virtually all of the Levittown people that I had grown up with. And over the years, I have lost my closest family members: my mother, Barbara, and my father, Edward Gray, and my sister, Bonnie. My trips to Levittown have dwindled to once every couple of years for a wedding or a christening or a first communion for one of my nephews or nieces. But when I do get back, I am happy to be there.

For me, the Legacy is something that you have to open yourself up to. And it is much more a series of successful training steps—physical and mental, growing into a proper use to increase an individual's drive and competitive nature.

And your coaches, if you are an athlete, are supposed to bring out your competitive nature in your sport, or mentors bringing it out in your practices. The 1960 and 1961 Levittown American coaches, with their 4-hours per day practices, did pretty well, even if the parents thought that the coach's practice schedule was crazy. But the coaches and the players and the parents wanted to win those World Championships and made sure that the 1960-61 players were going to play at a level that gave the Levittown American teams the best chance that it would happen.

And talking about coaching, the four Levittown high school's football coaches during the period from 1964-67, with their very high win/loss ratios, all performed admirably. I felt that my experience playing for Coach Dick Bedesem on the Bishop Egan City Championship teams was a great opportunity for me. Coach Bedesem was a *winner*. We won three Philadelphia Catholic League championships and two Philadelphia City Championships when I was playing there and the coaching was a very big reason that we succeeded.

And when I came to Penn State with Franco Harris and Lydell Mitchell and our teammates, we all were *winners*. Our aggregate Penn State win-loss records over the time period from 1968-1972 was 44 wins, 4 losses. I attribute a good part of that record to Joe Paterno, our head coach, who also was a *big-time winner*.

The town of Levittown and the environment that I grew up in, I now believe helped to lay the groundwork for all of our successes. Both the 1960 and 1961

Levittown American teams, with the competitive nature of the Levittown Legacy that I believe they possessed, performed at a level that showed people that a small group of young athletes can make a very large impression upon the rest of the sporting world!

Competition Matters! Viva Levittown American!

Appendix 1:
The 1960 Rules of Little League Baseball

In the Little League Official 1960 Rules and Regulations booklet which was published by Little League Baseball Inc., Williamsport, PA and sold for 10 cents ($0.10), the Rules and Regulations of Little League Baseball are broken down into a number of sub-headings below.

A.   **The League**

1) The League shall be governed by a Board of Directors consisting of all those ACTIVE in the Local League program.

2) The League shall be composed of not more than four (4) teams during its first year of operation and not more than six (6) teams thereafter.

3) Each League (Levittown had five different Leagues) shall apply for and, if approved, be issued a separate charter certificate.

4) Each league shall have separate boundaries as provided for. The League shall limit its boundaries to, and draw the players from, an area which includes not more than the population stipulated in Regulation IV (15,000 to start and later moved to 20,000).

B.   **Teams**

1) No team may have more than 15 players nor less than 12. The manager of the team must, at least five days prior to the first regularly scheduled game, register his regular team roster.

2) At no time a team shall have on its roster more than six players whose "League Age" is 12.

If the roster amounts to 12, it shall include not less than two players whose League Age is 10 or younger.

C.   Players

1) Any boy, who will attain the age of 13 before August 1 of the year in question, shall be ineligible to compete in Little League Baseball. This means that a boy who will be 13 years old, on August 1 or later is eligible to play that year; a boy who will be 13 years or older on July 31 or earlier, will not be eligible to play that year, and will not be eligible for either local league play or tournament play at any time during the calendar year in question.

2) Each candidate must present acceptable proof of age in the form of a birth certificate or hospital record to the league president at least 48 hours before the Player Auction is put into operation.

3) The President of the local league MUST certify and be responsible for the eligibility of each candidate.

4) The "League Age" of each candidate shall be recorded and announced at the player selection to guide the managers in making their decisions.

5) "League Age" is that age attained by a boy prior to August 1 in any given season. Thus, a boy whose 12th birthday is on July 31 or earlier has a League Age of 12; a boy whose 12th birthday is on August 1 or later has a League Age of 11.

6) Little League pitchers are limited to nine in-

nings in a game associated with the Little League
All-Star Tournament.

7) Girls are not eligible.

D. League Boundaries

1) Each league shall determine actual boundaries of the area from WITHIN which it will select
players. The boundaries MUST be described in
detail AND shown on a map.

2) The league shall limit its boundaries to and
draw its players from an area which includes not
more than a population of 15,000. The boundary
limitation later in the 1960's, would be increased to
a population of 20,000.

3) When there are two or more Leagues within
a locale (like Levittown), each must have separate
boundaries that are described in detail and shown
on a map.

E. The Playing Field

1) The distance between all bases shall be 60 feet.

2) The distance between the point of home plate
and the front side of pitcher's plate shall be forty-
six feet.

3) The Batter's Box shall be rectangular, five
feet six inches by three feet. The inside line shall
be parallel to and four inches away from the side
of home plate. It shall extend forward from the
center of home plate two feet six inches and to the
rear three feet.

4) The Pitcher's Mound shall be raised by a
gradual slope to a height of six inches above the
level of home plate and the base paths.

5)   Home plate shall be seventeen inches long on the edge the pitcher's mound and shall be seventeen inches from this side to the back point. The two sides shall be 8-1/2 inches long before then angle to the back point.

6)   The Pitcher's Rubber shall be four inches by eighteen inches.

7)   The Bases shall be 14 inches square not more than two and one-fourth inches high.

G.   Breaking the Rules

The Rules of Little League Baseball were designed in such a way that all the Little League teams and Little League All-Star teams would compete on a "level playing field". To take care of any age discrepancies local teams had to have a limited number of players, 12 to 15, with no more than 6 players whose League Age is 12, and not less than 2 players at League Age of 10.

Over Age: There is a limitation on "League Age" being less than 13-years old. To prove League Age, a player must possess proof of age—a birth certificate or hospital record. The age concern here is that one or several 13 to 15-year-old, younger-looking players in League Age may be added by an unscrupulous coach to the playoff roster for a Little League All-Star team. A problem for Little League Baseball administrators is, "How do you verify age?"

Non-Residence: This limitation is designed to prohibit players from switching from one local league, in which he is a resident, to another league, in which he is not a resident but may be living with a relative or friend to be eligible to play on a particular league's all-star team.

The Little League Baseball Tournament Eligibility Affidavit for the 1960 Levittown American League All-Star Team, shown as Appendix 2 below, lists the Names of Players, Street Address, Date of Birth, and Regular Season Team. The information is signed by: John R. Mack (President of Levittown American Little League).

So, what happens if and when you break the rules?

The two major concerns about eligibility are Age and Residence. In the 1992 Little League World Series, the Far East representative was from Zamboanga City in the Philippines. They used ineligible imported players, due to residence outside of the eligible area, to win the 1992 Little League World Championship against Long Beach, California by the score of 15-4. Due to the breaking of the rules by Zamboanga, Long Beach was declared the winner with a score of 6-0, and the Philippines had a very embarrassing forfeit.

Why can't girls play baseball?

The first girl known to have played Little League Baseball was Kathryn Johnston-Massar from Corning,

New York and she went by the nickname of "Tubby." She posed as a boy and played for King's Dairy.

It was 1951 and she cut her hair short and dressed like a boy and made the team and played first base and played it well. After making the team and part-way into the season, she told the coach that she was a girl. He said she was a good player and was wel-comed to stay. The Little League Board of Directors did not agree with Tubby's coach and she was not permitted to play Little League baseball. The "Tubby Rule" was created at Little League headquarters and it said, "Girls are not eligible under any circumstances."

In 1974, girls were finally allowed to play Little League Baseball, after contesting that position in numerous and costly court cases over the years. Still, not many girls try out to play on Little League baseball teams. The Van Aukens note that the Little League Softball program grew from approximately 30,000 players in 1974 to more than 390,000 play-ers when their book was published in 2001. And the Little League Rules ban against girl players was dropped from the Little League's Rules and Regula-tions in 1974.

Appendix 2:

Eligibility: Little League Baseball Tournament Team Eligibility Affidavit for 1960 American Little League: Levittown, PA

Name of Player	Address	DOB	Reg Season Team
Joseph Mormello Jr.	Bald Cypress Lane	1947	Watson & Schwartz
Joseph Fioravanti	Vermillion Drive	1948	Watson & Schwartz
Mark Griffith	Tulip Lane	1948	Watson & Schwartz
Chester Gardner Jr.	Vermillion Drive	1948	Richheimer
Donald Bickel	Vicar Lane	1947	Richheimer
James Grauel	North Court Lane	1948	Penn Fruit
Thomas Schwartz Jr.	Evergreen Lane	1947	Penn Fruit
Charles Barto	Twin Leaf Lane	1947	Halperin
Roland Clark	Morning Glory Ln	1948	Halperin
Craig Eisenhart	Magnolia Drive	1948	Halperin
Gary Saft	Primrose Lane	1948	Pomeroy
Brian Pennington	Tanglewood Lane	1948	Pomeroy
Julian Kalkstein	Teaberry Lane	1947	Lobel
James Flemin	Meadow Lane	1948	Lobel

Important: Unless supported by legal adoption or change of name documents, above players names must be the same as on proof of age documents. Players of League Age 11 and 12 only are eligible

Manager	Address	Season Team
William Dvorak	Turnhill Lane	Watson
Roger Witt	Lakeside Drive	Richeimer

I hereby certify that the dates of birth of the fourteen players listed above are correct and have been substantiated by Birth Certificate, Hospital Record or National Headquarters statement in lieu thereof.

I further certify that the players listed above reside within the League's boundaries as set forth in Regulation IV, and have been regular team members of the league for at least one-half of the regular season in accordance with TOURNAMENT RULES AND REGULATIONS.

Sworn before me this 14th day of July, 1960
Signed: John R. Mack (President)